MAKING OUT IN

JAPANESE

T0161116

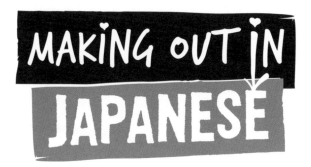

Revised Edition

Todd Geers and Erika Hoburg
revised by **Elisha Geers**

TUTTLE Publishing

Tokyo | Rutland, Vermont | Singapore

Published by Tuttle Publishing, an imprint of Periplus Editions (HK) Ltd.

www.tuttlepublishing.com

Copyright © 1988 Charles E. Tuttle Publishing Co. Inc.
Copyright © 2003, 2014 Periplus Editions (HK) Ltd.
Illustrations (full-paged) by Akiko Saito
All rights reserved.

LCC Card No. 88050165
ISBN 978-4-8053-1224-7

Distributed by:

Japan
Tuttle Publishing, Yaekari Building 3F
5-4-12 Osaki, Shinagawa-ku
Tokyo 141-0032, Japan
Tel: (81) 3 5437 0171
Fax: (81) 3 5437 0755
sales@tuttle.co.jp
www.tuttle.co.jp

North America, Latin America & Europe
Tuttle Publishing
364 Innovation Drive,
North Clarendon VT 05759-9436, USA
Tel: 1 (802) 773 8930
Fax: 1 (802) 773 6993
info@tuttlepublishing.com
www.tuttlepublishing.com

Asia Pacific
Berkeley Books Pte. Ltd.
3 Kallang Sector #04-01
Singapore 349278
Tel: (65) 6741-2178
Fax: (65) 6741-2179
inquiries@periplus.com.sg
www.tuttlepublishing.com

26 25 24 23
10 9 8 7 6   2303TP

Printed in Singapore

TUTTLE PUBLISHING® is a registered trademark of Tuttle Publishing,
a division of Periplus Editions (HK) Ltd.

Contents

Preface to the Third Edition

Thanks to you readers, ***Making Out In Japanese*** has long been a perennial favorite among people who want to boost their ability to jump in and converse. To help you keep it going, this new edition has eliminated some outmoded phrases and added some new ones. And because Japan, like the US, moves on a faster track than ever, we've added a chapter to help ensure your social savvy is up-to-date.

In a culture where social networking sites are growing increasingly popular, and having a cell phone (or two) is expected, being able to communicate about communicating has taken on an importance of his own. The realm of electronic communication has a constantly evolving and shifting *language* of its own, as well. The *Making the Scene* chapter includes a few terms and phrases to help you expand your virtual social network, decode the language of the Internet, and generally stay connected to your new friends, whether your preferred mode is a desktop computer or your smartphone.

We've also included new information on that other way to connect: face time. The not-so-new phenomenon of **gokon**, or a group date, is covered in the new chapter. (Not your usual date, it's competition, Japanese-style. Modesty is key, but don't be afraid to flaunt your **gaijin**-card.) This section shows you how to introduce yourself, how to make yourself sound more interesting and attractive than the next girl/ guy, and the protocol that can be expected after most **gokons** have been fleshed out. We'll also introduce you to some of the archetypes you'll see mostly in cities, but whose influence can be seen in less populated areas of Japan as well.

Some chapters now include a short vocabulary to help you get up to speed on some new and not-so-new terminology.

Have fun, and 頑張って！* **Ganbatte!**

* Hang in there!

Introduction

So no one understands your Japanese? Worse yet, you don't understand theirs. You've spent an entire week studying one phrase and you can't wait to use it. The big moment arrives—you're armed with the latest edition of *Learn Japanese in 27-and-a-½-Minutes-a-Day* for moral support—and you lay the phrase on some unsuspecting soul. What happens? The response isn't like the one in your book. Why?

Basically, because the Japanese don't "play by the book" just as Westerners don't "play by the book" when it comes to their daily language. So what to do? Well, you could quit and give up studying Japanese, or you could learn to speak real Japanese.

Just as we speak in a relaxed, colloquial manner, so do the Japanese. On trains, in clubs, during ball games, or with friends, they all use shortcuts in their speech. If you want to speak the way the Japanese speak, then you need to know what to say, how to say it, and when to say it.

And better still, you'll need to know the cultural context it all happens in. We've built in lots of little morsels in this book to help you build a picture of the real Japan as you go along. Right then? Okay, let's go!

INFORMATION

It's tricky to teach the proper pronunciation of a foreign language in a book, so we're not going to try, hoping you've already got the basics. To help you out, though, we've joined two and sometimes three or four words together, to make compound words or phrases that are easier to pronounce. Most of them are hyphenated to highlight merged words, to emphasize the slang suffixes and particles, and to facilitate pronunciation and memorization.

For example, the components of **fuzake-nai-deyo** (ふざけ ないでよ) are: **fuzake** (from **fuzakeru**), **nai-de** (command form of **arimasen**), and the (quite forceful) suffix **-yo**. We've written the compound phrase **fuzake-nai-deyo** so that you won't pause while pronouncing it, but say it entirely in one breath; a pause would weaken the impact.

We're sure that you're familiar with the polite question forms **des-ka** ですか and **mas-ka** ますか. Forget them. Except for a few needed for talking to strangers, requesting services, etc., the rest have been dismissed. In informal speech, rising intonation takes the place of these forms. Thus, the final syllables of all words and phrases in this book ending with a question mark should be pronounced with the kind of rising intonation we give to the question "Right?"

Slang that is too faddish is not included in this book, because such words come and go too quickly. If you use old slang, the reaction of your Japanese date will likely be, "He thinks he's being cool speaking like that, but nobody says that anymore. Hah, hah!" So we've avoided hot slang—if it's out of date people will think that you're funny or square. But feel free to use what you pick up on the street.

VARIATIONS

The terms "boy" and "girl" are used throughout the book, and we're definitely referring to the post-puberty phase here. To eliminate the embarrassing problem of boys using girls' words or vice versa, we've indicated words suitable for use by girls and boys with the symbols ♀ and ♂ respectively. Other words and phrases not marked can be used by both sexes, and (b→g) means a boy should use it when talking to a girl. For example:

Don't be upset.	**Okoranai-de.** ♂ 怒らないで。 **Okoruna-yo.** ♀ 怒るなよ。
Make me warm.	**Atatamete.** 暖めて。
You look beautiful.	**Kirei-dayo.** (b→g) きれいだよ。

But before you go thinking that boys' and girls' speech patterns are absolutely divided, stop a minute. Don't be shocked if you hear a girl using a quite masculine phrase (or vice versa). The gender gap in Japanese speech is narrowing, especially among young people, and there's nothing wrong with "borrowing" for impact or emphasis. In this book, we've made the distinction as a general guide to usage.

One thing you'll notice as you speak with the Japanese (especially if you move around) is that people's speech patterns vary wildly. We're not just talking about slang here, there are also big differences between regions and social groups. It's impossible for us to include all the variations (more on the regional ones later) of the phrases in this book, so we've gone a standard Japanese (**hyōjungo** 標準語) style, which everyone will understand and which you can adapt to the area you're living in.

Adaptation is really important—the phrases here might seem too harsh to some ears and too soft to others. Take your cues from the speech and reactions of people around you. If they warm to the way you're talking, great, otherwise think about the way they're taking it and adjust. If all else fails, ask—foreigners aren't expected to know everything!

JAPANESE-ENGLISH-JAPANESE-…

You'll have seen above that we've written Japanese phrases in two ways—in **rōmaji** (ローマ字—Western script, with lines above some vowels meaning long sounds) and in Japanese script with **furigana** (phonetic **hiragana** 平仮名 above the Chinese **kanji** 漢字) for an added challenge as you get better. But many phrases are written in another phonetic alphabet, **katakana** 片仮名. **Katakana** are mostly used for foreign words, and there are many of them in this book—for example, "batteries" are **batterī** バッテリー. Among other things, they're also used to write a few Japanese superlatives, such as **chō** 超 (ちょー)(amazing-ly/fantastic-ally).

When using **katakana**, life gets a bit tricky when you hit the limitations of the Japanese language. It has only one final consonant (**n**), so when the Japanese pronounce English words with other consonant endings, they have to tack on a vowel, usually a **u**. "Game" becomes **gēmu** ゲーム, "bed" becomes **beddo** ベッド, etc. With no final "r" sound, they usually use a long "a"; for example "locker" becomes **rokkā** ロッカー. And since there is no "l" at all, "r" is used instead.

There are a few introduced sounds that the Japanese can usually pronounce, and so they've created new ways of writing them. A "we" (as in "web") is written ウェ, and *v* sounds are written as ヴ followed by a **katakana** vowel, as in **va** ヴァ, **vi** ヴィ etc.—though the ability to pronounce the *v* varies greatly, especially between generations!

The Japanese enjoy using English words sporadically in their speech and you should do the same. With a little practice, it's easy to get the hang of how to "*katakana-ize*" an English word, that is, to pronounce it the way a Japanese would, strange as it might seem at first. As a foreigner, you'd be expected to use **katakana** words—so don't hold back!

As a reference point, the charts on pages 14 and 15 show the basic **kana** in each alphabet.

There are a few more variations in readings to watch out for. Notables are the use of **ha** as the subject particle, in which case it's read **wa** (such as 私は = **watashi-wa** = I am), and verbs ending in -**masu** ます, which we've romanized to -**mas**, because that's how you say it. You'll pick them all up as you go along.

THE BASIC HIRAGANA CHARACTERS

a あ	i い	u う	e え	o お
ka か	ki き	ku く	ke け	ko こ
ga が	gi ぎ	gu ぐ	ge げ	go ご
sa さ	shi し	su す	se せ	so そ
za ざ	ji じ	zu ず	ze ぜ	zo ぞ
ta た	chi ち	tsu つ	te て	to と
da だ	ji ぢ	zu づ	de で	do ど
na な	ni に	nu ぬ	ne ね	no の
ha は	hi ひ	fu ふ	he へ	ho ほ
ba ば	bi び	bu ぶ	be べ	bo ぼ
pa ぱ	pi ぴ	pu ぷ	pe ぺ	po ぽ
ma ま	mi み	mu む	me め	mo も
ya や		yu ゆ		yo よ
ra ら	ri り	ru る	re れ	ro ろ
wa わ				o を
n ん				

THE BASIC KATAKANA CHARACTERS

a ア	i イ	u ウ	e エ	o オ
ka カ	ki キ	ku ク	ke ケ	ko コ
ga ガ	gi ギ	gu グ	ge ゲ	go ゴ
sa サ	shi シ	su ス	se セ	so ソ
za ザ	ji ジ	zu ズ	ze ゼ	zo ゾ
ta タ	chi チ	tsu ツ	te テ	to ト
da ダ	ji ヂ	zu ヅ	de デ	do ド
na ナ	ni ニ	nu ヌ	ne ネ	no ノ
ha ハ	hi ヒ	fu フ	he ヘ	ho ホ
ba バ	bi ビ	bu ブ	be ベ	bo ボ
pa パ	pi ピ	pu プ	pe ペ	po ポ
ma マ	mi ミ	mu ム	me メ	mo モ
ya ヤ		yu ユ		yo ヨ
ra ラ	ri リ	ru ル	re レ	ro ロ
wa ワ				o ヲ
n ン				

BEING CHOOSY

There are plenty of phrases for which the Japanese have alternatives, as in any language. As well as the boy/girl classification, we've listed them in a rough order from least to most casual, also getting rougher as they become more casual. If what you're saying doesn't seem to fit the mood, again, adapt to the speech of the people around you!

In the book, we've included the Japanese words for "me" and "you" in many phrases. In practice, they often leave them out, unless particular clarification is needed, but until you can instinctively understand who is being referred to, it's best to use them. If you do, there are a range of words available, not just the gender-neutral **watashi** 私 (with its super-formal counterpart **watakushi** 私) and **anata** あなた that textbooks love.

For girls, there's **atashi** あたし, and for guys there's **boku** 僕 and **ore** 俺. To say "you," girls can say **anata** あなた or **anta** あんた, and guys can say **kimi** 君 or **omae** お前. In this book, we've stuck with **anata** and **kimi**, because these are the "safest" for everyday conversation. **Omae** and **ore** in particular are very harsh, uncompromising words that can put people off. Until you know when best to use these words (again by the speech of the Japanese around you), steer clear!

STRESSED OUT OVER ENDINGS

One thing that we have to say is that in Japanese, how you say something can have more meaning than what you say. Think about it: when you're sharing an intimate moment, you can convey many emotions by sounding caring and serious, on top of what you're actually saying. Some phrases can be changed from statements to questions just by the tone or particle at the end... the list goes on. Here's a run-down of some slang endings and tonal tricks.

For starters, the rules say that plain negative verbs end in **-nai** (e.g. **wakaranai** 分からない I don't understand/know). But you'll hear other forms, like **-n**, as in **wakaran** 分からん, or **shiran** 知らん (I dunno) or special corruptions like **wakan'nai** 分かんない and **iu** 言う pronounced **yū** ゆう. (Plain positive forms generally don't change as they're pretty simple already.)

The most common slang final particle is **ne**, often length-ened to **nē**. Only partly fictitiously, it seems to us that when a newborn Japanese baby is shown off for the first time, someone will say **Kawaii-nē?** かわいいねえ? (Isn't he/she cute?), and inevitably the flock of admirers will all say **Nē!** ねえ! (Oh yes!). From such early exposure, the child is doomed to utter **nē** for the rest of his/her life.

Nē gives an (familiar yet) emphatic ending, usually a rhe-torical question, and lengthening it adds more emphasis. With falling intonation it's more of an explanation. It isn't often said with a rising intonation, but can be said in a high pitch for emphasis. Girls prefer **ne** and **nē**, and guys have an alternative, **na**, which is used in the same way. But as we said before, the gap is narrowing, and, especially around women, guys will often use **ne**.

Other handy sentence endings (added to any form but the **mas** form) include **yo** よ, used to emphasize that "I'm telling you what I think (and you should do this)." **Wa** わ is often added by women to soften phrases, and you'll see it throughout this book. If you prefer a more blunt style, don't use it, or use **yo** instead. **-noda** 〜のだ (less formally **-nda** 〜んだ) makes the sentence a clear explanation, with a feeling, of "that's the way it is."

These can be combined liberally. For example, you're trying to decide which movie to see, and someone is being quite pushy about their choice. To be clear that you've already seen it and once was enough, you can say **Mō mitan-dayo-ne** もう見たんだよね。

Zo ぞ and **ze** ぜ can be added (usually by guys) to give instructions. **Zo** means "let's do..." as in **Yoshi, iku-zo** よし、行くぞ (Right, let's go), similar to but slightly harsher than **ikō** 行こう. **Ze** is a very strong command form, e.g. **Iku-ze!** 行くぜ! (Move it!) Finally, **-kke** is a handy ending, expressing either uncertainty or forgetfulness **Nan-datta-kke?** 何だったっけ? (What was it again...?)

The meaning of some phrases may be changed from a statement to a question by a rising final intonation, and these phrases are marked by diamonds (♦). For example:

Haven't seen you around for a while.	♦ **Hisashiburi-ne.** ♀ 久しぶりね。
	♦ **Hisashiburi-dane.** 久しぶりだね。

With a rising intonation, the sentence becomes "Haven't seen you around for a while, have I?"

And which parts of the phrase you stress also make a big difference—stressing a **yo** emphasizes that you're pushing your opinion. Stressing the **sō** in **sō-dane/sō des-ne** そうだね/そうですね (that's right) means you agree more strongly.

Finally, put emotion into your voice. You might think that the Japanese spoken around you is emotionless because it seems so fast, but nothing could be further from the truth. Put feeling into your voice as you would in English, and your message will be loud and clear.

THE LAST WORD

Does all of this sound really daunting? It shouldn't! Think of this introduction as a reference page for your journey through the Japanese-speaking world. Just keep these points in mind, and you'll find this book a valuable resource to speed your street Japanese skills along.

And there's one last thing: the Japanese love to see foreigners making an effort to speak Japanese! Through their troubles learning English, they know how hard it is, so even if you can't get the point across to start with, keep trying and you'll earn more respect. And if you're using real phrases like the ones in this book, all the better!

What have you been talking about?
Nani hanashiteta-no?

What's wrong?
Dō shita-no?

What's happening?
Nani-ka atta-no?

Nothing much.
Betsu-ni nani-mo.

I'm (a bit) depressed.
(Chotto) ochikonderu.

Thank you!
Arigatō!

That's tough!
Taihen-dane!

It'll work out.
Nantoka naru-yo.

Cheer up!
Genki dase-yo!

What's Up?

Hello! Hi!

Ohayō!
おはよう！
Kon'nichi-wa!
こんにちは！
Konban-wa!
こんばんは！

Ohayō! is used in the morning, say until 10 a.m., and with people you're seeing for the first time that day. **Kon'nichi-wa!** is for the daytime, and **Konban-wa!** for the evening. As everyday phrases, there are many variations and contractions of these, formal and informal, and they differ between regions of Japan—but these are the universal standards!

Haven't seen you around for a while.

Hisashiburi.
久しぶり。
Hisashiburi-dayo-ne.
久しぶりだよね。

This is the first of many overused phrases you'll come across in this book; **Hisashiburi** is a natural and integral part of a greeting to someone you haven't seen for a while.

How are you?	**Genki?** 元気？
How's it going?	**Genki datta?** 元気だった？
	Saikin dō? Genki? 最近どう？元気？
So we've met again.	**Mata atta-ne.** また会ったね。
I wanted to see you/ I missed you.	**Aitakatta.** 会いたかった。

You can use this to a friend (as in "I missed you") or to your lover (as in "I was lonely without you"), though naturally you'll put more feeling into the latter. It can also be used about a third person.

How have you been doing (recently)?	**(Saikin) Dō shiteta?** (最近)どうしてた？
	(Saikin) Nani shiteta? (最近)何してた？
What have you been doing?	**Nani yatteta-no?** 何やってたの？

Usually for asking what's happened just before or just recently (e.g. in the last week).

What's up?

Nan-ka kawatta-koto atta?
何か変わったことあった？

Not used as a first greeting, and more appropriate for someone you haven't seen for a while (e.g. a week, a month), especially if you think something might have changed. It literally means "Has something special (unusual) happened to you?" Answers could be **Betsu-ni** 別に, **Nani-mo** 何も ("Nothing much"), or a description of whatever has happened.

What's happening?

Dō shita-no?
どうしたの？

You know what's going on, but you missed a bit of it.

Nani-ka atta-no?
何かあったの？

For when you don't know what's going on.

What have you been talking about?

Nani hanashiteta-no?
何話してたの？

Nothing much.

Betsu-ni nani-mo.
別に何も。

Betsu-ni.
別に。

Nani-mo.
何も。

Toku-ni (nai)
特に（ない）。

Nothing special.   **Betsu-ni kawan'nai.**
別に変わんない。

Aikawarazu.
相変わらず。

Okay, I guess.   **Anmari.**
あんまり。

I'm fine.   **Genki.**
元気。

Genki-yo. ♀
元気よ。

Genki-dayo. ♂
元気だよ。

Māne.
まあね。

So-so/Not good,   **Mā-mā.**
not bad.   まあまあ。

What's wrong?   **Dōka shita-no?**
どうかしたの？

Nan-ka atta-no?
何かあったの？

These are general enquiries about whether something is wrong, in a situation where you haven't noticed any particular problem.

Dō shita-no?
どうしたの？

Asking this shows that you are much more sure (than with the above two phrases) that something is wrong, and so it should be voiced with more concern.

Dō shitan-dayo? ♂
どうしたんだよ？

You ask this when there is clearly a problem, e.g. if the other person suddenly stops talking in the middle of a conversation.

I'm really busy (with work/university).	(Shigoto/Daigaku-de) tottemo isogashii. (仕事・大学で) とっても忙しい。
I'm (a bit) sick.	(Chotto) byōki-da. (ちょっと) 病気だ。
I've got a cold.	Chotto kaze(-o) hi'iteru. ちょっと風邪 (を) ひいてる。
I'm (a bit) depressed.	(Chotto) ochikonderu. (ちょっと) 落ち込んでる。

I'm tired.	**Tsukareteru/Tsukareta.** 疲れてる/疲れた。

Tsukareteru is used in the general sense, whereas **Tsukareta** is more commonly used after an event or a hard day's work.

I'm sleepy.	**Nemui.** 眠い。

I'm not sleepy.	**Nemuku-nai.** 眠くない。

That's a bummer/tough!	**Taihen-dane!** 大変だね! **Taihen-dana!** ♂ 大変だな!

This is a classic Japanese expression of sympathy, disappointment, frustration. It's very flexible, and how you voice it adapts it to the situation. An understanding tone conveys sympathy with the other person's problems, or by adding force you show frustration with your own problems, which you can emphasize by making it **Taihen-dayo!** 大変だよ!

That can't be helped/ **There's nothing you** **can do about it.**	**Shikata (-ga) nai-ne.** 仕方(が)ないね。

That's unfortunate/ **That's a shame.**	**Zan'nen-dane.** 残念だね。

Along with **Taihen,** these are more overworked phrases. **Shikata nai-ne** especially expresses a sense of helplessness—"A decision has been made higher up, and it's final." A sympathetic tone shows that you share the other person's feelings.

It'll be okay/	**Nantoka naru-yo.**
It'll work out.	何とかなるよ。
Cheer up!	**Genki dashite!**
	元気出して!
	Genki dase-yo! ♂
	元気出せよ!

These sorts of phrases will suffice for most greetings. The Japanese tend not to go into a lot of detail nor openly say what they think, especially in simple conversations, unless they're really excited or frustrated etc. Take your cues from those around you about how elaborate your explanations should be—as much as you can, fitting in is important!

What's on your mind?	**Nani kangaeten-no?**
	何考えてんの?
Nothing.	**Betsu-ni.**
	別に。
	Nan-demo nai-yo.
	何でもないよ。
	Nani-mo.
	何も。

Nan-demo nai-yo is a response to "What's wrong?" or "What's on your mind?" **Nani-mo** is a response to many questions, showing that there's nothing on your mind, that you don't want to say anything, or there's nothing happening.

I was just thinking. **Kangae-goto shiteta.**
考え事してた。

These answers show that you were thinking, but don't have anything to say about it.

Chotto-ne.
ちょっとね。

Chotto-ne shows that you were thinking, and invites the other person to ask about it.

I was just daydreaming. **Bōtto shiteta.**
ぼーっとしてた。

Leave me alone! **Hottoite!**
ほっといて！

It's none of your business! **Kankei nai-desho!** ♀
関係ないでしょ！

Kankei nai-darō! ♂
関係ないだろう！

Yokei-na osewa!
よけいなお世話！

Is Sally okay? **Sarī genki?**
サリー元気？

How's Sally doing?　　　Sarī dō shiteru?
サリーどうしてる?

The answer to **Sarī genki?** will usually be "She's okay." and the answer to **Sarī dō shiteru?** will usually be "She's okay. She has been doing. . ." **Genki. . . shiteru** 元気<ruby>げんき</ruby>...してる。 or "She's okay. She went to..." **Genki... ni itta** 元気<ruby>げんき</ruby> ... に行った<ruby>い</ruby>。 **Dō shiteru?** should solicit a longer answer.

Seen Jeff?　　　Jeffu minakatta?
ジェフ見<ruby>み</ruby>なかった?

I saw/met Kerry.　　　Kerii-ni atta.
ケリーに会<ruby>あ</ruby>った。

I want to see you soon.　　　Sugu(-ni) aitai.
すぐ(に)会<ruby>あ</ruby>いたい。

See you later.　　　Jā mata-ne.
じゃあまたね。

Mata-ne.
またね。

Mata.
また。

Goodbye.　　　Sayōnara.
さようなら。

Bai-bai.
バイバイ。

No.
Iya,...

Yes.
Hai.

Really?
Maji?

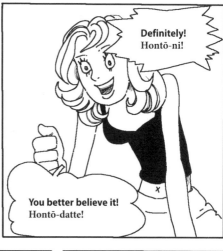

Definitely!
Hontō-ni!

What?
E?

You better believe it!
Hontō-datte!

This is too good
to be true!
Uso-mitai!

That's it!
Sore-dayo!

I'm not interested.
Kyōmi nai-yo.

Because...
Datte...

No way!
Jōdan-ja nē-yo!

2

Yes and No

Yes.	**Hai.**
	はい。
	Ee.
	ええ。
	Un.
	うん。

There are many ways to indicate agreement in Japanese, and these are the most direct. **Un** and **Uun** (see below) are very casual and natural, and they especially should be accompanied with gestures to make yourself clear.

No.	**Iie.**
	いいえ。
	Uun.
	ううん。
	Iya,...
	いや、…

Iya is often used before another phrase, to explain or soften the disagreement, such as **Iya**, **betsu-ni** いや、別に "no, not especially."

The Japanese, following their preference for indirectness, don't always say "yes" and "no" in the Western sense.

That's right!	◆ **Sō-dane!**
	そうだね！
	◆ **Sō-dana!** ♂
	そうだな！
	Mā-ne!
	まあね！

Mā-ne is often used to mean "I know." If said teasingly, it means "Yeah I know (but I might not tell you)." For example: "She's pretty, isn't she? Do you know her?" "Maybe I know her, maybe I don't." (**Mā-ne**.)

I think so too.	**Sō omou.**
	そう思う。
	Sō-yo-ne. ♀
	そうよね。
	Sō-dayo-ne.
	そうだよね。
I agree (!)	**Sansei (!)**
	賛成（！）
So am I/Me too.	**Watashi-mo.** ♀
	私も。
	Boku-mo. ♂
	僕も。

I see/I got it/ **I understand.**	Naruhodo.
	なるほど。
	Wakatta.
	分かった。
	Aa, sō-ka.
	ああ、そうか。
	Sokka.
	そっか。
	Sō, sō…
	そう、そう…

Sō, sō… in particular is often used just to mean "I'm listening to you and understanding what you're saying." You'll soon pick up from the speech patterns of those around when they're questioning you with a variant of **so** and when they're just letting you know they're listening.

All right, that's OK.	Okkē.
	オッケー。
	Daijōbu(-dayo).
	大丈夫(だよ)。
No problem.	Mondai nai-yo.
	問題ないよ。

Colorful conversations can be created by injecting more than just a "yes" or "no." Study the following words and phrases. They can be voiced inquisitively or doubtfully, depending upon your tone of voice.

Really?	Hontō?
	本当?
	Hontō-ni?
	本当に?

Maji-de?
マジで？

Maji?
マジ？

Uso/Ussō?
うそ？／うっそー？

Is that so? **Sō-nano?**
そうなの？

Sō?
そう？

This has to be the most overused phrase in Japanese! Again, sometimes it just means "I'm listening to you" and sometimes it's used to ask for clarification etc. Non-verbal cues will tell you!

Did you/Do you/ **Sō-nano?**
Are you? そうなの？

Yeah, I know (groaned). **Sō-nanda-yo-nē.**
そうなんだよねえ。

For example: "Your car is no good!" **Kono kuruma-wa dame!** この車はだめ！ "Yeah, I know." **Sō-nanda-yo-nē.**

He/She/It seemed **Sō-mieta-yo.**
like one/that. そう見えたよ。

I guess so. **Sō-da-to omou.**
そうだと思う。

Sō-dane.
そうだね。

It might be true.	Sō-kamo-ne. そうかもね。
Maybe.	Tabun-ne. 多分ね。
Maybe not.	Chigaun-ja nai-(no). 違うんじゃない(の)。
That's not right.	Son'na-koto nai-yo. そんな事ないよ。
I wonder...	Sō-ka-nā... そうかなあ…
I don't think so/ I doubt it.	Sō omowanai. そう思わない。
I'm not sure.	Yoku wakaranai. よく分からない。
There's no way of knowing.	Wakaru-wake nai-yo. 分かる訳ないよ。
I can't say for sure.	Nan-to-mo ienai. 何とも言えない。 Hakkiri ienai. はっきり言えない。
Because...	Datte... だって…

Datte is usually followed by an explanation.

But...   Demo...
                          でも…

Usually followed by an explanation or a contradiction, such
as "but, that's wrong." **Demo chigau-yo.** でも、違うよ。

Here are some handy phrases for when you want to put
questions back to the other speaker.

How come?   Nan-de?
                          何で?

                          Dō shite?
                          どうして?

                          Dō shite-dayo?
                          どうしてだよ?

What do you mean?   Dō-iu imi?
                          どういう意味?

Is something wrong/   Kanji-ga chigau-yo-ne.
different? (because   感じが違うよね?
you seem different)   Kanji-ga chigaun-dakedo.
                          感じが違うんだけど?

You can ask this when the other person seems a bit different (e.g. from the last time you saw them).

                          (Anoko,) Nan-ka chigau-
                          ne?
                          (あの子、)何か違うね?

This is useful when a third person seems a bit different.
Anoko means "That (young) person over there."

Nan-ka chigau-no?
何か違うの?

This is more suited to asking about things, not people.

What's the difference?	**Dō chigau-no?** どう違うの?
What?	**Nani?** 何? **E?** え?
Why not?	**Nan-de (dame-nano)?** 何で(だめなの)? **Nan-de dame-nanda-yo?** ♂ 何でだめなんだよ?
Are you serious?	**Honki?** 本気?
Are you sure?	**Hontō-ni?** 本当に? **Zettai?** 絶対?

Zettai? is a much more emphatic way to ask. **Hontō-ni?** is a safer bet in most situations. Clip the final **ni** for more emphasis.

You don't mean it? **(You're joking?)**	**Jōdan-desho?** 冗談でしょ? **Jōdan-darō?** ♂ 冗談だろう?

But, of course, there are times when you want to make your point forcefully. Here are some words and phrases that will help you make a bigger impact. Just be careful with the negative ones!

Absolutely!	**Zettai!** 絶対！
Definitely!	**Hontō-ni!** 本当に！
	Hontō-ni sō-dayo-ne! 本当にそうだよね！
	Hontō-ni sō-dayo-na! ♂ 本当にそうだよな！
	Maji-de. マジで。

When using **Majide** to mean "Definitely," you can lengthen the final **e** sound, but don't raise the intonation (as with "Really?")

Of course!	**Atarimae-deshō!** 当たり前でしょう！
	Atarimae-dayo! ♂ 当たり前だよ！

Used in the sense of "That goes without saying!"

	Mochiron! もちろん！

Usually used as an answer to a question.

You better believe it!	**Hontō-datte!** 本当だって!
	Hontō-dayo! 本当だよ!
That's it!	**Sō-yo!** そうよ!
	Sore-yo! ♀ それよ!
	Sore-dayo! ♂ それだよ!

These phrases point out the best choice among (tangible or intangible) alternatives, e.g. after a question like "Which one?" **dore?** どれ?

That was good.	♦ **Yokatta (yo)-ne.** よかった(よ)ね。
Right on! (Great!) **I did it!**	**Yatta!** やった!
	Yoshi! ♂ よし!
	Ii-zo! ♂ いいぞ!
You're kidding me!	**Karakawanai-de!** からかわないで!
	Uso-bakkari! うそばっかり!
	Uso-bakka! うそばっか!

These phrases are commonly used by the Japanese, so don't confuse **bakka** (a short form of **bakkari** meaning "only" or "just") with **baka** ばか ("fool," an especially harsh insult in Osaka). For more emphasis, you could lengthen the last syllable or the **kk** pause of **bakkari**, or clip the last syllable of **bakka**.

This is too good to be true!	**Uso-mitai!** うそみたい！
No way/Stop joking! (a strong refusal)	**Jōdan-ja nai-wayo!** ♀ 冗談じゃないわよ！
	Jōdan-ja nē-yo! ♂ 冗談じゃねえよ！
That's wrong!	**Chigau-wayo!** ♀ 違うわよ！
	Chigau-yo! ♂ 違うよ！
That's impossible!	**Dō-shiyō-mo nai-wayo!** ♀ どうしようもないわよ！
	Dō-shiyō-mo nai-yo! どうしようもないよ！
	Shikata-ga nai-yo! 仕方がないよ！
	Muri! 無理！
	Muri-yo! ♀ 無理よ！
	Muri-dane! ♂ 無理だね！

Forget it!   Mō ii-yo!
(I've had enough!) もういいよ！

Bullshit!   Yoku iu-yo!
                        よく言うよ！

Literally means "How dare you say that!"

I don't care.   Dō-demo ii-yo.
(Anything's fine.) どうでもいいよ。

                        Kamawanai.
                        かまわない。

It means nothing to me. Kankei nai-wa. ♀
                             関係ないわ。

                             Kankei nai-yo.
                             関係ないよ。

I'm not interested.   Kyōmi nai-wa. ♀
                             興味ないわ。

                             Kyōmi nai-yo. ♂
                             興味ないよ。

3

Got a Minute?

Got a minute?	Jikan aru? 時間ある? Chotto ii? ちょっといい?
Till when?	Itsu-made? いつまで?
(About) when?	Itsu-(goro)? いつ(ごろ)? Itsu-(gurai)? いつ(ぐらい)?
About what time?	Nanji-goro? 何時ごろ?
Is it too early?	Haya-sugiru? 早過ぎる?

Is it too late?　　Mō osoi?
　　　　　　　　　　もう遅い?

This "too late" refers to events in the past or now, e.g. **Eiga-o mi-ni iku?** 映画を観に行く? ("Shall we go see the movie [now]?") **Aa, mō osoi.** ああ、もう遅い。 "Oh, it's too late." because it's already started.

　　　　　　　　　　Oso-sugiru?
　　　　　　　　　　遅すぎる?

This "too late" refers to events in the future, e.g. "Shall we go to the 11 o'clock movie?" **Jū-ichiji kara eiga-o miyō?** １１時から映画を観よう? **Aa, (owari-wa) oso-sugiru.** ああ、（終わりは）遅すぎる。 "Oh, it'll end too late." [because the trains will have stopped running so we can't get home etc.]

When is it convenient　　Itsu-ga ii?
for you?　　　　　　　　いつがいい?

How about the 18th?　　Jū-hachi-nichi-wa dō?
　　　　　　　　　　　　　１８日はどう?

Then when can you　　　Itsu-nara ii?
make it?　　　　　　　　いつならいい?

　　　　　　　　　　　　　Itsu aiteru?
　　　　　　　　　　　　　いつ空いてる?

You have already said **Itsu-ga ii** いつがいい? and maybe even **Jū-hachi-nichi-wa** １８日は? and they still can't decide.

What time can I come over?	Nanji-ni kureba ii? 何時に来ればいい？
What time do we leave?	Nanji-ni iku? 何時に行く？ Nanji-ni deru? 何時に出る？
What time do we arrive?	Nanji-ni tsuku? 何時に着く？

The Japanese reputation for punctuality is well-earned. Suffice to say that if you make a promise to do something, especially as most people take public transport and have to plan accordingly, you should stick to your word! Dependability is highly valued in Japan, so if you can't make it on time, get in touch via mobile phone (see *On The Phone*).

Are you ready?

Yōi dekita?
用意できた?

Mada?
まだ?

Ii?
いい?

When will you do it?

Itsu suru?
いつする?

Itsu yaru-no?
いつやるの?

How long will it take?

Dono-gurai kakaru?
どのぐらいかかる?

Next time.

♦ Kondo-ne.
今度ね。

Maybe later.

Tabun kondo.
多分今度。

You will do it, but you don't know/haven't decided when.

Later.

Ato-de.
後で。

You'll do it a few hours or so later.

♦ Sonouchi-ni-ne.
そのうちにね。

You'll do it a few days or weeks later. Alternatively, you may not want to do it and are fobbing someone off—this is a vague expression.

Soon.

Mō-sugu.
もうすぐ。

Not yet.

Mada.
まだ。

Not now.

Ima-ja nakute.
今<ruby>今<rt>いま</rt></ruby>じゃなくて。

The last time (you did something).

Kono mae.
この前<rt>まえ</rt>。

Kono aida.
この間<rt>あいだ</rt>。

Konaida.
こないだ。

I don't know when.

Itsu-(da)ka wakaranai.
いつ(だ)か分<rt>わ</rt>からない。

I don't know now.

Ima chotto wakaranai.
今<rt>いま</rt>ちょっと分<rt>わ</rt>からない

I don't know yet.

Mada (chotto) wakaranai.
まだ(ちょっと)分<rt>わ</rt>からない

Someday.

Itsu-ka.
いつか。

Not next time.

Kondo-ja nai.
今度<rt>こんど</rt>じゃない。

Kondo-ja naku.
今度<rt>こんど</rt>じゃなく。

Anytime is fine.	Itsu-demo ii-yo. いつでもいいよ。
Always.	Itsumo. いつも。
You decide when.	Itsu-ka kimete. いつか決めて。 Jā kimete. じゃあ、決めて。
That's a bad day for me.	Sono hi-wa (chotto) dame. その日は（ちょっと）だめ。
That day is fine.	Jā sono hi-ne. じゃあ、その日ね。 Iiyo! いいよ！

Iiyo! said positively means "That's fine!" Don't say it negatively or glumly, or it'll mean "I've had enough" (see *Yes and No*).

Let's begin!	Hajime-yō! 始めよう！ Jā yarō! じゃあ、やろう！
It'll only take a minute.	Sugu-dakara. すぐだから。

Let's continue.	Tsuzuke-yō! 続けよう！
Do it later.	Ato-de shite. 後でして。
I'll be finished soon.	Sugu owaru. すぐ終わる。
I've finished.	Owatta. 終わった。 Dekita. できた。

Both of these are very common phrases, but **Dekita** only applies to something that has a clear start and finish, such as cooking dinner, a project or homework, but not work, which carries on the next day, and so isn't "finished" in the same sense. **Owatta** can apply to anything, including work. The limitation to **Dekita** also applies below.

Finished?	Owatta? 終わった？ Dekita? できた？
Finished already?	Mō owatta? もう終わった？ Mō dekita? もうできた？

4

Say What!

Listen.	Ki'ite. 聞いて。
Listen to me.	Chotto ki'ite. ちょっと聞いて。 Ki'ite-yo. 聞いてよ。
Don't listen/ Don't ask me (that).	Kikanai-de. 聞かないで Kikuna-yo. ♂ 聞くなよ
Did you hear me/ him/them?	Kikoeta? 聞こえた?
I couldn't hear.	Kikoenakatta. 聞こえなかった。

I didn't hear.	**Kikanakatta.** 聞かなかった。
I don't want to hear.	**Kikitaku-nai.** 聞きたくない。
Speak up.	**Motto ōkii-koe-de hanashite.** もっと大きい声で話して。
Speak more slowly.	**Motto yukkuri itte.** もっとゆっくり言って。
Please speak slower.	**Mō chotto yukkuri shabette.** もうちょっとゆっくりしゃべって。
Say it again.	**Mō ikkai itte.** もう一回言って。 **Mō ichido itte.** もう一度言って。

With sentences such as these, which are essentially requests often voiced as statements, it's softer to use a rising intonation and/or add **kureru?** くれる? to the end of the sentence. If you use a falling intonation the request is harsher, more like an order. Women especially should use this with care.

Let's talk in Japanese.	**Nihongo(-de) hanasō.** 日本語(で)話そう。
Let's talk in English.	**Eigo(-de) hanasō.** 英語(で)話そう。

It's a cliché, but the Japanese are generally ashamed of their English-speaking ability. The Japanese school system teaches them very precise and technical grammar, but not how to speak. Even those who go to **Eikaiwa** 英会話 (private English conversation schools) aren't very good, or confident even if they are. A sure-fire way to get the conversation bubbling is to use the following two stock phrases.

| **You're good at English.** | **Eigo jōzu-(da)ne.**
英語上手(だ)ね。
Eigo umai-ne.
英語うまいね。 |

This will usually be followed by an embarrassed denial. To show that you really mean it, say...

| **Yes, you really are good.** | **Un, jōzu-dayo.**
うん、上手だよ。
Un, umai-yo.
うん、上手いよ。 |

Even if you carry on in Japanese, you'll have made a good impression!

| **Where did you learn/ are you learning English?** | **Doko-de eigo-o benkyō shita/shiteru-no?**
どこで英語を勉強した／してるの？ |

| **How long did you learn/have you been learning English?** | **Dono-gurai eigo-o benkyō shita/shiteru-no?**
どのぐらい英語を勉強した／してるの？ |

To prolong the topic of conversation, and to make a Japanese person feel really good about his/her English, you can ask if he/she has been overseas.

Have you studied English overseas/in America/in the UK?	Gaikoku/Amerika/Igirisu-de (eigo-o) benkyō shita koto aru? 外国／アメリカ／イギリスで (英語を) 勉強 したことある？

If they have, and elaborate a little, you can say "That's great" **sugoi-ne** すごいね . If they haven't, the classic ingratiating reply is to express surprise and reiterate that their English is fantastic.

But your English is so good!	Demo, eigo (sugoku) jōzu-ne! ♀ でも、英語(すごく)上手ね。 Demo, eigo (sugoku) umai-ne! 英語(すごく)うまいね。

By the way, a foreigner who speaks even a little Japanese will be constantly praised in ways like this. This is just one reason it's good to make an effort!

Say something.	Nan-ka itte. 何か言って。

What are you talking about?	Nani hanashiteru-no? 何話してるの?
	Nani itten-no? 何言ってんの?
	Nani itten-dayo? ♂ 何言ってんだよ?

The last two are more accusative, and are especially used when you want to oppose or criticize the speaker.

| **Let's keep talking about it.** | Hanashi-o tsuzuke-yō.
話を続けよう。 |
| | Motto hanasō.
もっと話そう。 |

| **Let's talk about it later.** | (Sore-wa) ato-de hanasō.
(それは)後で話そう。 |

| **Can we talk about this later?** | Kono-koto-wa mata ato-de hanasō?
このことはまた後で話そう? |

| **I don't want to talk.** | Hanashitaku-nai.
話したくない。 |

| **I don't want to talk about it.** | Sore-ni tsuite hanashitaku-nai.
それについて話したくない。 |
| | Mō sono-koto-wa hanashitaku-nai.
もうそのことは話したくない。 |

By the way...	Tokoro-de... ところで...
Just to change the subject...	Chotto hanashi-ga kawaru kedo... ちょっと話が変わるけど...

Before the conversation is about to zoom off into the realms of unpleasantness, there are a few ways you can try to lighten the mood. A good one is the "crazy foreigner" routine. The Japanese are fond of onomatopoeias, words that imitate sounds, and used at the right moment, the following will produce a laugh or three.

dog barking	wan-wan ワンワン
cat meowing	nyan-nyan ニャンニャン
light rain	shito-shito シトシト para-para パラパラ
heavy rain	zā-zā ザーザー
light crying	shiku-shiku シクシク

Rub your eyes while saying **shiku-shiku**.

heavy crying

en-en
エンエン

walking noise

teku-teku
テクテク

(beer) drinking noise

goku-goku
ゴクゴク

sucking noise

sū-sū
スースー

I'm hungry.

Onaka-ga peko-peko.
おなかがペコペコ。

My head feels dizzy.

Atama-ga fura-fura.
頭がフラフラする。

I have a sharp pain in my stomach.

I-ga kiri-kiri itai.
胃がキリキリ痛い。

But then again, sometimes even the best comics have to put their foot down...

Don't make excuses.

Iiwake shinai-de.
言い訳しないで。

That's not a good excuse!

Sore iiwake-janai!
それ言い訳じゃない！

Stop complaining!

Butsu-butsu iwanai-de! ♀
ブツブツ言わないで！

Butsu-butsu iu-na! ♂
ブツブツ言うな！

Monku bakka(ri) iu-nayo! ♂
文句ばっか（り）言うなよ！

Do you know what you're saying?

Nani itten-no?
何言ってんの？

This, voiced with incredulity, implies that the other person is saying crazy things.

Nani itten-no-ka wakatten-no?
何言ってんのか分かってんの？

This is harsh! It's a sure bet to enrage the other person. If they are talking rubbish it'll put them in their place, but be careful!

You said that, didn't you?

Sō itteta-kke?
そう言ってたっけ？

Sō itta-yone?
そう言ったよね？

Sō itteta-deshō? ♀
そう言ってたでしょう？

So itteta-darō? ♂
そう言ってただろう？

Sō itteta-kke? means "I don't remember, but I think you said that, right?" It can also be used about yourself, such as "Oh, did I say that?" It and **So itta-yone?** are part "I don't remember…" and part accusative, and pronunciation will show the difference. The last two are outright accusative, and should be used with caution.

I didn't say anything. Nani-mo ittenai-yo.
何も言ってないよ。

This sentence is in the general sense, such as in response to "Did you spread the latest rumor?"

Nani-mo iwana-katta.
何も言わなかった。

This sentence should be used about a particular subject and/or communication to one person, such as "Did you tell her my secret?"

You shouldn't say things like that. Son'na-koto iwanai-hō-ga ii-yo.
そんな事言わない方がいいよ。
Son'na-koto itcha-dame-yo. ♀
そんな事言っちゃだめよ。
Son'na-koto itcha-dame-dayo. ♂
そんな事言っちゃだめだよ。

The last two sentences are quite harsh, sitting close to the following in forcefulness.

Don't say things like that. Son'na-koto iuna-yo. ♂
そんな事言うなよ。

Don't talk so loudly. Son'na-ni ōkii-koe-de shaberanai-de/hanasanai-de.
そんなに大きい声でしゃべらないで／話さないで。

DIFFICULTY COMMUNICATING

These are some phrases to help you communicate when you feel like you aren't expressing yourself clearly. There will be moments of confusion, pain, and frustration, but you can express those feelings in the hope that your partner will step up his or her game and try to listen with eyes as well as ears.

Tell me what you're thinking.	Nani kangaeteru-ka oshiete. 何考えているか教えて。
I'm confused.	Konran shiteru. 混乱してる。
I don't understand.	Yoku wakaranai. 良く分からない。
I don't understand what you're trying to say.	Nante iō-to shiteru-ka wakaranai. 何て言おうとしてるか分からない。
I can't explain it.	Umaku setsumei dekinai. 上手く説明できない。
I'm sorry I can't explain it well.	Umaku setsumei dekinakute gomen. 上手く説明できなくてごめん。

I'm sorry that I can't understand what you're trying to say to me.	Nante itteru-ka wakatte agerarenakute gomen. 何て言ってるか分かってあげられなくてごめん。
I wish my Japanese/ English was better.	Motto (watashi-no ♀/boku-no ♂) Nihon-go/Ei-go-ga umakattara... もっと(私の／僕の) 日本語／英語が上手かったら…
This is difficult to talk about.	Umaku ienai. 上手く言えない。
This is so frustrating.	Ira-ira suru. イライラする。
I can't understand you if you talk so fast.	Son'na-ni hayakuchi-de shabettara nante itteruka wakaranai そんなに早口でしゃべったら何て言ってるか分からない。
What do you mean by that?	Dō-iu imi? どういう意味？

5

Comings and Goings

Come here.

Chotto kite.
ちょっと来て。

Come over.

Oide-yo.
おいでよ。

Come over later.

Ato-de kite.
後で来て。

Can you come?

Koreru?
来れる?

Won't you come with us/me?

Issho-ni konai/kuru?
一緒に来ない／来る?

She/He is coming here.

Kanojo/kare-mo kuru-yo.
彼女／彼も来るよ。

I'm coming, wait a second.

Ima iku.
今行く。

I can go.	**Ikeru.** 行ける。
I think I can go.	**Ikeru-to omou.** 行けると思う。
I can't go.	**Ikenai.** 行けない。
I want to go.	**Ikitai.** 行きたい。
I want to go to Tokyo.	**Tōkyō(-e/ni)-ikitai.** 東京 (へ／に)行きたい。
I really want to go.	**Hontō-ni ikitai.** 本当に行きたい。 **Chō-ikitai.** 超行きたい。
I don't want to go.	**Ikitaku-nai.** 行きたくない。
I really don't want to go.	**Hontō-ni ikitaku-nai.** 本当に行きたくない。
You went, didn't you?	**Itta-deshō?** 行ったでしょう？ **Itta-yo-nē?** 行ったよねえ？ **Itta-yo-nā?** ♂ 行ったよなあ？

Ittan-deshō? ♀
行ったんでしょう？

Ittan-dayo-nē?
行ったんだよねえ？

The last two phrases are more positive, as in "I know you went (because she told me)!"

I went.	**Itta.** 行った
I didn't go.	**Ikanakatta.** 行かなかった。
Don't go.	**Ikanai-de.** 行かないで。 **Ikuna-yo. ♂** 行くなよ。
Don't go yet.	**Mada ikanai-de.** まだ行かないで。 **Mada ikuna-yo. ♂** まだ行くなよ。
I must go now.	**Ikanakucha.** 行かなくちゃ。
May I go?	**Itte-mo ii?** 行ってもいい？
Shall we go?	**Iku?** 行く？

Let's go.   **Ikō.**
                                 行こう。

                                 Sā, ikuka.
                                 さあ、行くか。

                                 Mō ikō.
                                 もう行こう。

Mō ikō is said if you should leave because of the time, as in "We should go now or we'll be late."

Let's leave/   **Mō de-yō.**
get out of here.   もう出よう。

Said only when inside a building, car etc.

I'm leaving soon.   **Mō-sugu deru.**
                                 もうすぐ出る。

She/He has left here.   **Kanojo/kare itchatta-yo.**
                                 彼女／彼行っちゃったよ。

She/He has gone home.   **Kanojo/kare kaetchatta-yo.**
                                 彼女／彼帰っちゃったよ。

Stay here.   **Koko-ni ite.**
                                 ここにいて。

Where are you going?   **Doko iku-no?**
                                 どこ行くの？

Please go first/   **Osaki-ni dōzo.**
After you.   お先にどうぞ。

                                 Saki-ni dōzo.
                                 先にどうぞ。

| **Thanks for letting me go first** | Saki-ni gomen-ne.
先にごめんね。 |

| **Take your time (go slowly).** | Yukkuri itte.
ゆっくり行って。 |

| **I'm lost.** | Michi-ni mayotta.
道に迷った。 |

This is used when you've lost your way.

Wakaranai.
分からない。

This is used when you don't understand.

| **Please tell me the way.** | Iki-kata-o oshiete-kusasai.
行き方を教えてください。 |

| **Could you write it down?** | Kaite-kureru?
書いてくれる？ |

There are many transport options in Japan, but (for most purposes) the trains (**densha** 電車) are by far the best. They are clean, air-conditioned and impeccably punctual, so you can plan your itinerary to the minute if you want! There are lines serving almost all parts of the country, with the famous **Shinkansen** (新幹線 bullet trains) for fast inter-city trips, subways (**chikatetsu** 地下鉄) criss-crossing the cities and regular trains in between. Trains, especially the **Shinkansen** and **tokkyu** (特急 limited expresses) can often be quite expensive, but for ultra-reliable mass transportation they can't be beaten.

Buses (**basu** バス) are good for short trips around town and the suburbs, but the traffic congestion hampers their reliability. Highway buses (**haiweibasu** ハイウェイバス) are a cheap way to get between major cities, many running overnight, but again, crowded roads mean that the time-tables are a rough guide only. Planes (**hikōki** 飛行機) are a good choice for inter-island (especially to Hokkaido, where there is no **Shinkansen** 新幹線) and long-distance travel, but prices vary (train prices are constant) so it pays to book early.

And like many things, cars (**kuruma** 車) are expensive in Japan, with a myriad of taxes and laws adding cost and hassle. Unless you're living in an isolated area, it's much easier to get around on public transport. The system can be daunting, but the ticket vending machines are all essentially the same and all signs are written in romaji, so once mastered, it's easy. Here are some key phrases to help you ask the way.

Don't forget (to tell me) the train station names.	Eki-mei-o wasurenai-de. 駅名を忘れないで。
Which train/bus should I take?	Dotchi-no densha/basu? どっちの電車／バス？
Where do I get off?	Doko-de oriru-no? どこで降りるの？
Get off at … (station/bus stop).	…eki/basutei-de orite. 駅／バス停で降りて。

Eki ("station") is added to the proper name of some stations, but not to all, e.g. **Kyōto-eki** 京都駅, **Hanshin Umeda** 阪神梅田, etc.

How will I know when to get off?	**Itsu oriru-ka, dō shitara wakaru-no?** いつ降りるか、どうしたら分かるの？
(It's OK), you'll hear the station name on the PA.	**Anaunsu-de ekimei-ga nagareru. (Daijōbu-dayo.)** アナウンスで駅名が流れる。(大丈夫だよ。)
(About) how much does it cost?	**Ikura (gurai) kakaru-no?** いくら(ぐらい)かかるの？
I'll be waiting at the ticket gate/the station office/by the ticket machines/in front of the station/at the bus stop.	**Kaisatsu-guchi/eki'in-shitsu/kippu-uriba/eki-mae/basutei-de matteru.** 改札口／駅員室／切符売り場／駅前／バス停で待ってる。
hotel	**hoteru** ホテル
airport	**kūkō** 空港

6

Eat, Drink, Be Merry

Eating and drinking are vital parts of socializing in Japan. With relations at work often quite hierarchical and stiff, going out and relaxing becomes very important to relieve stress and tension. Even within a relaxed university environment, people still enjoy the liveliness of alcohol and food-fueled conversation.

There are many special occasions when the Japanese will eat out or have a big meal in. Apart from birthdays, family occasions like after students' graduations (from every school) and the **seijinshiki** 成人式 (coming-of-age ceremony at age 20, held on the second Monday in January), and work-centered events like **hanami** 花見 ("flower viewing" or drinks under the cherry trees in March/April) are ideal times to get together over some food and drink.

For a description of going out options, see *Check it Out*, and for ways to chat up the opposite sex, see *Making the Scene* and *Chit Chat*. For strictly food-related phrases, read on.

I'm hungry.	**Onaka(-ga) suita.** おなか(が)すいた。 **Hara hetta.** ♂ 腹へった。
I'd like to eat something.	**Nan-ka tabetai.** 何か食べたい。
I haven't eaten yet.	**Mada tabetenai.** まだ食べてない。
Do you want to eat?	**Tabetai?** 食べたい？
I don't want to eat.	**Tabetaku-nai.** 食べたくない。
I won't eat.	**Tabenai.** 食べない。
Did you eat lunch/ dinner?	**Gohan tabeta?** ご飯食べた？ (Did you eat?) **Hiru-gohan** 昼ご飯 (lunch) **Ban-gohan** 晩ご飯 (dinner)
What would you like?	**Nani-ga hoshii?** 何が欲しい？

Used more in a shopping context.

Nani-ga ii?
何_{なに}がいい？

Best suited to eating contexts.

What's that?	**Nani sore?** 何_{なに}それ？
Not that.	**Sore-ja nakute.** それじゃなくて。
Do you want to eat some more?	**Motto taberu?** もっと食_たべる？
I'm thirsty.	**Nodo(-ga) kawaita.** のど（が）乾_{かわ}いた。
I'd like a beer/wine/ chūhai.	**Bīru/wain/chūhai(-ga) nomitai.** ビール／ワイン／チューハイ（が）飲_のみたい。

Chūhai are alcoholic drinks based on **shōchū**, a kind of Japanese vodka. They come in at about 5%, in sweet and sour flavors and are easy to drink—but bite hard the next day! To avoid hangovers (**futsukayoi** 二日酔_{ふつかよ}い) you could settle for the following.

I'd like a soft drink/cola/melon soda/juice/coffee/tea/green tea.	Sofuto dorinku/kōra/meron sōda/jūsu/kōhī/kōcha/ocha(-ga) nomitai. ソフトドリンク／コーラ／メロン・ソーダ／ジュース／コーヒー／紅茶／お茶が飲みたい。
I don't want to drink.	Nomitaku-nai. 飲みたくない。
I won't drink.	Nomanai. 飲まない。
I can't drink.	Nomenai. 飲めない。
I haven't drunk yet.	Mada nondenai. まだ飲んでない。
Do you want to drink something?	Nan-ka nomu? 何か飲む？
Do you want to drink some more?	Motto nomu? もっと飲む？
Thank you, but I still have some.	Arigatō, demo mada aru-kara. ありがとう、でもまだあるから。

Drink a little bit more.	**Mō-sukoshi non-de.** もう少し飲んで。
	Mō-chotto non-de. もうちょっと飲んで。
	Mō-choi non-de. もうちょい飲んで。
How about (some) dinner?	**Shokuji shinai?** 食事しない？
	Gohan taberu? ご飯食べる？

Note that when talking about meals, **gohan** (literally "rice") is more commonly used in informal situations than **shokuji** (literally "meal").

Is the meal ready?	**Shokuji dekita?** 食事できた？
	Gohan mada? ご飯まだ？
It's ready.	**Dekita.** できた。
Have you ordered?	**Chūmon shita?** 注文した？
	Tanonda? 頼んだ？

When visiting someone's house/eating a meal they've cooked, respect for the food (and hence their feelings) is the watchword! Here is a huge array of unusual (to Western eyes) food in Japan, and you sometimes get the feeling that your hostess will cook a few particularly unusual things for you to try. You're generally not expected to like everything, but you must try things—such an adventurous spirit is admired in Japan!

Will you try this (food)?	**Tabete-miru?** 食べてみる？
Try this!	**(Kore) tabete-mite!** (これ)食べてみて！
What's it called?	**Nante iu-no?** 何て言うの？
I've never tried...	**...tabeta-koto nai.** ...食べたことない。

Even if you've been in Japan for a while and your hosts know that, expect to be asked what your favorite Japanese food is, and whether or not you can eat the more challenging varieties. It's just something you have to get used to as a stepping stone to more interesting food-related conversation.

What's your favorite Japanese food?	**Nihon-no tabemono-de, nani-ga ichiban suki?** 日本の食べ物で、何が一番好き？

| **Can you eat nattō/anko?** | **Nattō/anko taberareru?** 納豆／あんこ食べられる？ |

Nattō is fermented soybeans, which are stringy and foul-smelling. **Anko** is the general name for sweet soybean paste, and like **nattō** is often unpalatable to foreigners, hence the Japanese often asking if you can eat them.

| **Yes, I can.** | **Un, taberareru(-yo).** うん、食べられる（よ）。 |

| **No, I can't.** | **Uun, taberarenai.** ううん、食べられない。 |

There is no shame whatsoever in saying this! Of course, you could also say that you've never tried it: **Tabete-mita koto-ga nai** 食べてみたことがない。 But that might prompt your hosts to offer you some!

| **(That) looks delicious.** | **(Are) oishisō.** （あれ）おいしそう。 |

| **It smells good.** | **Ii nioi.** いい匂い。 |

| **Give me a bit more.** | **Mō sukoshi.** もう少し。 **Mō chotto.** もうちょっと。 |

| **Gimme more.** | **Motto chōdai.** もっとちょうだい。 |

That's enough.	**Jūbun.** 充分。 **Tariru.** 足りる。
Enough?	**Tarita?** 足りた？
Not enough.	**Tarinai.** 足りない。
(Sorry,) I can't eat that.	**(Sumimasen,) Sore tabe(ra)renai.** (すみません)それ食べ(ら)れない。
Itadakimas!	**Itadakimas!** いただきます！

Almost every Japanese says this before eating, in almost any situation. The closest English equivalent is "grace," but it has lost its religious meaning (of receiving from the gods). Don't hesitate to say this before a meal, and you may even be complimented on your good manners!

Does this taste good?	**Kore oishii?** これおいしい？
It tastes good.	**Oishii (!)** おいしい（！）

This is another grossly overworked word, which can be voiced with the full gamut of emotions, from excited enthusiasm to indifference (meaning that it may not be good at all!). The Japanese tend not to be specific about what they think of the texture or flavor—they just show how they feel about it by how much emotion they put into saying **oishii**. You can add other words, such as **kekkō oishii** 結構おいしい ("It's really good" even without much enthusiasm), but just saying **oishii** and meaning it is usually enough.

It's an unusual taste.	**Fushigi-na aji-dane.** 不思議な味だね。

It's okay/So-so.	**Mā-mā.** まあまあ。

These two are also polite ways of saying you don't really like something, especially if it's something the other person has made. (If they're really proud of it, it's best to say **oishii** but be less enthusiastic than normal). The following three phrases are also handy, but best left for eating out, where you won't be insulting anyone by criticizing the food!

It's not good.	**Yoku-nai.** よくない。

It doesn't taste good.	**Oishiku-nai.** おいしくない。

It's awful.	**Mazui.** まずい。 **Hidoi.** ひどい。

I'm full.	Onaka(-ga) ippai. お腹(が)いっぱい。
I'm done!/Thank you for a wonderful meal.	Gochisōsama(-deshita)! ごちそうさま(でした)!

This is the end-of-meal counterpart to **itadakimas**. It literally means "It was a feast," and is a sign of appreciation.

JAPANESE EATERIES

As in most places, there are so many types of eateries in Japan that the word restaurant just doesn't cover it. Here are a few different places where you can grab a bite.

tachigui sobaya/ 立ち食いそば屋 stand-and-eat noodle restaurant (clearly not for leisurely dining. This is a place where you eat and run.)

izakaya/ 居酒屋 Japanese-style drinking house (These places are great for after-work drinking. They generally serve casual foods that go well with alcoholic beverages. More on **izakaya** in *Check it Out*.)

kaiten zushi/回転寿司 conveyer belt sushi restaurant (In these places dishes of food are placed on a conveyer belt that goes through the restaurant and around the tables. Diners grab whatever plates take their fancy.)

famirī resutoran/ ファミリーレストラン (**fami-resu** ファミレス for short) This is the Japanese equivalent of a diner

kissaten/喫茶店 (or **kafe/cafe** カフェ) coffee house

konbini/ コンビニ convenience store

depachika/ デパ地下 a deli in the basement level floor of a department store

bā or **pabu** or **sunakku/** バー、パブ、スナック a bar/pub

7

The Way I Feel

I like it.	**Suki.** 好き。 **Suki-dayo.** 好きだよ。
I like it a lot.	**Dai-suki.** 大好き。 **Dai-suki-dayo.** 大好きだよ。
I love it!	**Mecha-mecha suki!** メチャメチャ好き!

Metcha is an Ōsaka slang word meaning "very" that has caught on nationwide.

It's OK/so-so.	**Mā-mā.** まあまあ。
I don't like it very much.	**Anmari suki-ja nai.** あんまり好きじゃない。

If someone is offering you something but you really don't want it, say this to avoid hurting their feelings. **Mā-mā** is a politer way of saying this.

I hate it.	**Suki-ja nai.** 好きじゃない。 **Kirai.** 嫌い。 **Kirai-dayo.** 嫌いだよ。
I hate it a lot.	**Dai-kirai.** 大嫌い。 **Dai-kirai-dayo.** 大嫌いだよ。
I really hate it.	**Hontō-ni/Maji-de kirai.** 本当に／マジで嫌い。

The Japanese tend not be too open about what they don't like. Using anything below **suki-ja nai** is really firing off verbal bullets—pick your target carefully!

I want...(object).	**...-ga hoshii.** …が欲しい。
I really want...(object).	**Chō/Hontō-ni/Maji-de ...-ga hoshii.** ちょー／本当に／マジで …が欲しい。
I want...(action).	**...-ga shitai.** …がしたい。

I really want…(action).	**Chō/Hontō-ni/Maji-de … -ga shitai.** ちょー／本当に／マジで …がしたい。
I don't want…(object).	**Ii.** いい。 **Iranai.** いらない。 **Hoshiku-nai** 欲しくない。
I really don't want/ need…(object).	**Hontō-ni/Maji-de iranai.** 本当に／マジでいらない。 **Hontō-ni/maji-de hoshiku-nai.** 本当に／マジで欲しくない。
I don't want…(action).	**Iya.** いや。 **Yada.** やだ。 **Yada-yo.** やだよ。
I really don't want… (action).	**Hontō-ni/Maji-de… shitaku-nai.** 本当に／マジで…したくない。

The Japanese usually differentiate between wanting an object (noun) and wanting action (verb). The distinction isn't absolute—you will hear **…shitehoshii** …して欲しい ("I want to do…")—and it varies between speakers and regions, but we'll keep it simple here.

If you want an object (for example, chewing gum), place the noun in front of **ga hoshii**. E.g. **Gamu-ga hoshii** ガムが欲しい (I want some gum.) If you want an action (to go), add **tai** to the verb (stem form). E.g. **Ikitai** 行きたい (I want to go.)

The negative form works in much the same way, just changing the final **-i** to **-ku-nai**. E.g. **Gamu-ga hoshiku-nai** ガムが欲しくない (I don't want any gum.) Or, more commonly but less politely, you can just say **Iranai** いらない (I don't want/need [it]).

For not wanting an action, add **taku-nai** to the verb stem. E.g. **Ikitaku-nai** 行きたくない (I don't want to go), **shitaku-nai** (I don't want to do it), or you can just say **Iya**, **Yada**, or **Yada-yo** (I don't want [to]). Because these last three are already rough slang, they should not be said harshly, or their meaning would be too strong.

Ii is for either objects and actions, but can indicate wanting as well as not wanting something, depending on how it is voiced. A falling intonation and negative gestures means no, and with enthusiastic delivery plus positive gestures it means yes. This is a common word that needs great care!

I'm busy.	**Isogashii.** 忙しい。
I'm happy.	**Ureshii.** (joyous) うれしい。 **Shiawase.** (fortunate) 幸せ。

I'm happy to hear that. Sore-o ki'ite ureshii.
それを聞いてうれしい。

I'm glad to know that. Sore-o ki'ite yokatta.
それを聞いてよかった。

I'm sad. Kanashii.
悲しい。

I'm fine. Genki.
元気。

I'm mad/I'm mad at you! Atama-ni-kita!
頭にきた！

Atama-kita!
頭きた！

Atama-kuru!
頭くる！

For these phrases, **atama** is pronounced differently than when said by itself. It should be said quickly, in a staccato manner, such as **ah-tah-mah-**... And usually these phrases are said jokingly; if you tell your wife that she's "silly," she'll definitely reply **Atama-kita!**

I'm ready. Yōi dekita.
用意できた。

I'm tired. Tsukareta.
疲れた。

I'm freaked. Bibitta.
びびった。

I'm surprised! **Odoroita!**
驚いた！

Bikkuri shita!
ビックリした！

Bikkuri shita is more common, and a more natural exclamation.

What a relief. **Hotto shita.**
ほっとした。

Yokatta.
良かった。

I'm relieved **Anshin shita.**
(to hear that). 安心した。

I'm scared. **Kowai.**
怖い。

I feel sick. (That's) **Kimochi warui.**
sickening/Yuck. 気持ち悪い。

I'm disappointed. **Gakkari shichatta.**
ガッカリしちゃった。

Gakkari shita-yo.
ガッカリしたよ。

I was worried. **Shinpai shita.**
心配した。

I can do it. **Dekiru-yo.**
できるよ。

Can you do it?	Dekiru? できる？
I can't do it.	Dekinai. できない。
Can't you do it?	Dekinai-no? できないの？
I can't help it/ That can't be helped.	Shikata nai-yo. 仕方ないよ。 Shō-ga nai-yo. しょうがないよ。
Sorry, I can't.	Warui-kedo dame. 悪いけどだめ。 Warui-kedo dame-da. ♂ 悪いけどだめだ。
I should do it/ I gotta do it.	Shinakucha. しなくちゃ。 Yaranakucha. やらなくちゃ。
I'll do it.	Atashi-ga suru. ♀ あたしがする。 Atashi-ga yaru. ♀ あたしがやる。 Boku-ga suru. ♂ 僕がする。 Boku-ga yaru. ♂ 僕がやる。

I'm tired of it.	Mō akite kichatta. もう飽きてきちゃった。
	Mō akita. もう飽きた。
I understand.	Wakatta. 分かった。
Yeah yeah.	Hai hai はいはい。
I understand very well.	Yoku wakatta. よく分かった。
I think I understand.	Wakatta-to omou. 分かったと思う。
I don't understand.	Wakaranai. 分からない。
I don't understand very well.	Yoku wakaranai. よく分からない。
I know.	Wakatteru. 分かってる。
	Shitteru. 知ってる。

Wakatteru, which is used mostly for actions, means "Even if you didn't mention it, I knew that." Or "Okay, I'll do it, so stop your nagging!" E.g. "Go and clean your room." **Wakatteru.** (I know I need to do it.) "The party starts at 7 p.m." **Wakatteru.** (I know [because I already heard about it].) **Shitteru** can be used for objects and actions. E.g. "I know (her)" and "I know (how to get there)." **Shitteru.**

I know that person.	Ano hito shitteru. あの人知ってる。
Do you know that?	Sore shitteru? それ知ってる？
Ah, you know that.	Aa, shitten-da. ああ、知ってんだ。
I don't know.	Shiranai. 知らない。
I didn't know.	Shiranakatta. 知らなかった。
I didn't know that, though.	Shiranakatta-kedo. 知らなかったけど。
You know (knew) that, don't (didn't) you?	Shitteru (Shitteta)-deshō? 知ってる(知ってた)でしょう？
Give me time to think it over.	Kangae-sasete. 考えさせて。
I'll think about it.	Kangae-toku-yo. 考えとくよ。
I'm so confused.	Atama-ga kongaragatta. 頭がこんがらがった。
	Nanda-ka yoku wakaranai. 何だかよく分からない。

Mō wakan'nai!
もう分かんない!

I made a mistake.   Machigaeta.
間違えた。

I blew it.   Shippai shita.
失敗した。

Am I right?   Atteru?
あってる?

Am I wrong?   Machigatteru?
間違ってる?

Atteru? and **Machigatteru?** are used to clarify whether or not what you've said or done was right.

What a pity!   Kawaisō!
かわいそう!

Too bad.   Okinodoku.
お気の毒。

◆ Hidoi-ne.
ひどいね。

◆ Hidoi-na. ♂
ひどいな。

These may all be used in a sympathetic or sarcastic context, depending upon your tone of voice.

I hope so.   Sō-dato ii-ne.
そうだといいね。

It's risky!

Yabai!
やばい！

Go! Go for it!
(Good luck!)

Ganbatte!
頑張って！

Ganbare!
頑張れ！

Ganbare! is stronger, and is used in any situation (speaking directly to someone who is about to sit a test/play sport, cheering for your favorite team, encouraging runners in a marathon etc). **Ganbatte** is usually only used when speaking directly to someone. When used before the event, these phrases are the normal Japanese equivalent to "good luck."

Kintama doko-ni tsuiteru-no? ♂
金玉どこに付いてるの？

This literally means "Where are your balls?" Guys can use this to other guys if they aren't trying very hard in a sports match or in picking up girls.

Calm down!

Ochitsuite!
落ち着いて！

Asen'na-yo! ♂
あせんなよ！

Cheer up!

Genki dashite! ♀ (g→b)
元気出して！

Genki dase-yo! ♂
元気出せよ！

Never mind.   **Ki-ni shinai-de.**
気にしないで。

Ki-ni sun'na-yo. ♂
気にすんなよ。

Cool.   **Kakkoii.**
かっこいい。

Said especially about boys and cars.

Uncool.   **Dasai.**
ダサい。

This is an abbreviation of **Datte, Saitama no...** だって、埼
玉の… ("But, that's from Saitama"), a phrase first used by
downtown Tokyo-ites, meaning that something comes
from the unfashionable outer suburb of Saitama.

Really cool.   **Saikō.**
最高。

Maji-de kakkoii.
マジでかっこいい。

Chō kakkoii.
ちょーかっこいい。

Awesome.   **Sugoi.**
すごい。

Sugē. ♂
すげえ。

Cute.   **Kawaii.**
かわいい。

Kawaii is more commonly said by girls.

Really cute.　　　　　　**Chō kawaii.**
　　　　　　　　　　　　　ちょーかわいい。

　　　　　　　　　　　　　Sugoku kawaii.
　　　　　　　　　　　　　すごくかわいい。

If there's one thing you must understand about the world of Japanese romance, it's the power of "cute," and in Japanese it has a much broader meaning than just small fluffy things. Say tennis is in fashion, but you don't know how to play. It's not really important because, come spring, like all style-conscious Japanese, you must carry a tennis racket everywhere. It doesn't matter how well you play, what counts is that you have a cute cover for your racket, preferably with three Mickey Mouse patches and some English words. And the English should not make sense—something like "Active Sports: Traditional Mind for Specialty" would do nicely.

Clever/smart.　　　　　♦ **Atama ii-ne.**
　　　　　　　　　　　　　頭 いいね。

　　　　　　　　　　　　　♦ **Kashikoi.**
　　　　　　　　　　　　　かしこい。

Copycat.　　　　　　　**Manekko.**
　　　　　　　　　　　　　まねっこ。

Ugly.　　　　　　　　　**Kakko warui.**
　　　　　　　　　　　　　かっこ悪い。

　　　　　　　　　　　　　Dasai.
　　　　　　　　　　　　　ダサい。

What's your job?
Shigoto nani shiten-no?

A good-looking young man
Ike-men

I'm a hairstylist.
Biyōshi desu.

I'm at a Starbucks in Shinjuku now.
Shinjuku-no Sutaba nau.

This app is really useful, isn't it?
Kono apuri benri dayo-ne?

Do you mind if I smoke?
Tabacco suttemo daijōbu des-ka?

Maid Cafes
meido kafe

pretty
kirei-me

Guy as frivolous
Charai

I'm a salaryman.
Sararīman desu.

Do you have Facebook?
Feisu-bukku yatteru?

Do you want to exchange mail?
Meado/renraku-saki kōkan shinai?

Once I get home, I'll upload these pictures, ok?
Ie-ni kaettara kono shashin apu suru-ne?

8

Making the Scene

As we mentioned in *Eat, Drink, Be Merry*, there comes a time for stepping out of the rigidness of the workplace and enjoying time with friends, co-workers and family. The next three chapters are all about getting seriously social. This chapter shows you some of the newer ways of making the social scene.

SOCIALIZING WITH TECHNOLOGY

There's a certain amount of Facebook and Twitter use in Japan but, by and large, Japanese prefer their home grown media sites, and are less about using social media to keep up with friends than they are about interacting with communities that share their particular interests, like gaming communities and art sharing sites. It's a good way to commune with people who are into the same things you are. Here are some terms and phrases you may run into on the social networking scene.

feisu-bukku フェイスブック Facebook

tsuittā ツイッター Twitter

mixi, a Japanese social networking site. It used to be invitation-only, but now anyone can register for an account. Unlike Facebook, it is more focused on "journal entries", "communities", than, although available, event sharing or photos. It's easier to stay anonymous on a site like this, and most Japanese prefer it that way.

tsubuyaku つぶやく to give your status update. Literally to "say" or "murmur".

ii-ne! いいね! to "like" something on a social networking site (i.e. Facebook, mixi, Twitter, etc).

burogu ブログ blog

nau なう transliteration of "now". Used for updates on where one is, or checking in.

I'm at a Starbucks in Shinjuku now.	Shinjuku-no Sutaba nau. 新宿のスタバなう。

appu アップ to upload

Once I get home, I'll upload these pictures, ok?	Ie-ni kaettara kono shashin appu suru-ne? 家に帰ったらこの写真アップするね?

apuri アプリ app(lication) for smart phones

This app is really useful, isn't it?	Kono apuri benri dayo-ne. このアプリ便利だよね。
This app kinda sucks.	Kono apuri anmari yoku-nai-yo. このアプリあんまり良くないよ。
I don't understand how to use this, will you teach me?	Tsukaikata yoku wakara-nai, oshiete-kureru? 使い方良く分からない、教えてくれる?
What kind of phone do you have?	Don'na keitai tsukatteru? どんな携帯使ってる?
Do you have a Facebook (account)?	Feisu-bukku yatteru? (♀/♂) フェイスブックやってる?
Can I have your "mail" address?	Meado chōdai? (♀/♂, but more feminine than masculine) メアドちょうだい?
Do you want to exchange mail addresses/contact info?	Meado/renraku-saki kōkan shinai? (f/m) メアド／連絡先交換しない?

**Will you text me?
(as in, I would like it
if you text me.)**

Mēru shitte?
メールして？

**Let's (exchange
information via)
infrared beams!**

Sekigaisen shiyō!
赤外線しよう！

---

sumāto-fon スマートフォン smart phones

keitai-bangō (kei-ban) 携帯番号（携番）cellphone number

mēru メール (n.) a text message (not SMS), or (v.) to text/email someone on your phone (not SMS).

meado メアド cellphone email address. Short for メールアドレス **mēru adoresu**

sekigaisen 赤外線 a method of exchanging information on cellphones via transmitting and receiving infrared rays to each other's phones.

shame 写メ a photo email via cellphone. Short for **shashin mēru** 写真メール (picture email) or **shamēru** 写メール

ww: only used when typing, it's a slang that is on par with lol or haha. Also typed as "笑"、which is the kanji for "laughter"

GOKON: (GROUP DATING)

This is a very popular way to meet people in Japan. Basically, a mix of men and women get together for dinner and drinks. Generally, at least one person in the group is meeting another for the first time. Usually there are romantic expectations, but more and more people are participating in these **gōkons** 合コン just to meet people and have a good time. The phrases below work for group dates, at parties, or just getting to know (or pick up) someone else.

What's your name?	**Namae nante iu-no?** 名前何て言うの?
Guess what it is!	**Atete mite!** 当ててみて! **Nan-da-to omou?** 何だと思う?

You might hear these two if you ask a personal question. Either they're playing with you or they really don't want you to know. You have to read their body language!

My name is _____.	_____ **desu.** ♀/♂ _____です。
Where do you live?	**Doko-ni sunderu-no?** どこに住んでるの?
Where do you come from?	**Dokkara kita-no?** どっから来たの?

Doko-ni sunderu-no? should be used if you are introduced by someone. If there is no introduction, both **Doko-ni sunderu-no?** and **Dokkara kita-no?** are okay and both produce the same answer. Girls might tell you which city/area they live in, or they may just say **atchi** あっち, meaning "Over there."

How old are you?	**Nansai?** 何歳？

To this question, girls will usually answer with **Atete! Nansai-da-to omou?** 当てて！何歳だと思う？ Guess! How old do you think I am?, or **Ikutsu-ni mieru?** いくつに見える？ How old do I look?

What's your job?	**Shigoto nani shiten-no?** 仕事何してんの？

I'm working as an OL (pronounced like the letters, "O,L.") **Office Lady.** (A generic title for women working an administrative job)	**OL yatte masu.** ♀ OL やってます。

I'm a salaryman. (a generic title for a man working an office job)	**Sararīman desu.** ♂ サラリーマンです。

Are you a student?	**Gakusei?** 学生？

The answer might be **daigakusei** 大学生 (university student), **senmon-gakkōsei** 専門学校生 (student of a specialist school e.g. dental assistant, nurse etc).

Where are you studying (i.e. at what institution)?	**Doko-de benkyō shiteru-no?** どこで勉強してるの？

I'm a student.

Gakusei desu.
学生です。

I'm an art (college) student.

Bidaisei desu.
美大生です。

I'm a technical school student.

Senmon-gakkōsei desu.
専門学校生です。

I'm a teacher/instructor.

Kyōshi desu.
教師です。

I'm a hairstylist.

Biyōshi desu.
美容師です。

I work with computers.

IT(ai-tī)-kei no shigoto-o shiteimasu.
ＩＴ系の仕事をしています。

I'm from _____ (hometown), but now I live in _____. (city/area)

_____ shusshin desu-ga, ima-wa _____-ni sunde-imasu.
_____ 出身ですが、今は _____ に住んでいます。

When I was a student, I_____.

Gakusei-no toki-wa_____ -o yatte-imashita.
学生の時は_____ をやっていました。

played in a band/ **bando**/ バンド

played soccer/ **sakkā**/ サッカー

played American Football/ **american futtobōru (ame-futo)**/ アメリカンフットボール（アメフト / **Ame-futo** for short)

Basketball/ **basuketto-bōru (basuke)**/ バスケットボール（バスケ /**basuke** for short)

was on the swim team/ **suiei**/ 水泳

was on the track team/ **rikujō**/ 陸上

I like to _____
during my free time.

Shumi-wa _____desu.
趣味は_____です。

karaoke/ **karaoke**/ カラオケ

surfing/ **sā-fin**/ サーフィン

cycling/ **saikuringu**/ サイクリング

golf/ **gorufu**/ ゴルフ

shopping/ **kaimono**/ 買い物

finding new cafes/ **kafe meguri**/ カフェ巡り

going to art galleries/ **bijutsukan meguri**/ 美術館巡り

working on my car/ **kuruma-no mentenansu**/ 車のメンテナンス

guitar/drums/piano/trumpet/ **gittā/doramu/**

piano/toranpetto/ ギター、ドラム、ピアノ、トラン
ペット

going to concerts/ **konsāto-e iku-koto/** コンサート
へ行く事

play video games/ **gēmu/** ゲーム

I prefer the outdoors/ indoors/	Autodoa-ha/indoa-ha desu. アウトドア派／インドア派です。
How long have you been in Japan?	Nihon-ni kite-kara dono-kurai? 日本に来てからどのくらい？
I've lived in Japan for _____ months/years.	Nihon-ni sunde _____ kagetsu-me/ nen-me desu. 日本に住んで_____ケ月目／年目です。
I'm not shy.	Hitomishiri-wa amari shinai-hō-desu. 人見知りはあまりしないほうです。
Do you mind if I smoke?	Tabacco suttemo daijōbu des-ka? タバコ吸っても大丈夫ですか？

(A lot of restaurants and bars allow smoking inside, but it is still polite to ask the people around you if it's okay that you smoke.)

Look for more lines and other conversation carriers in *Chit Chat*.

SOME COMMON EXPRESSIONS

When you're out on the scene, you'll hear a lot of expressions that don't have a real English translation. On the other end of the scale you might hear one or two that are borrowed from English. This is just a handful of expressions you might hear on a regular basis.

oyobi/ お呼び／ booty call—literally, "an invitation." The slang use of this word usually has randy connotations, but in other contexts it's just any ordinary invitation/ request/call.

fumidai/ 踏み台 rebound—literally, a step stool. In the West, a rebound is most often a post-breakup relationship you jump into to avoid being alone. In Japan a rebound is more like that household tool you step onto to reach for bigger and better things, so to speak. (Example: Cut it out! He's not my boyfriend, he's just a rebound.)

nonke/ ノンケ This is a term used within the gay community to refer to straight people, but not used within the mainstream (i.e. straight) society to refer to each other. You can also say **sutorēto**/ ストレート straight or **nōmaru**/ ノーマル "normal." You might hear both, but it's better not to use **nōmaru** for the same reason you wouldn't call a straight person "normal" and a gay person "abnormal" outside of Japan. If you are asked if you are **nonke**, you might have wandered into 2-Town! (Incidentally, to experience gay night life in Tokyo, head for the **ni-chōme**/ 二丁目 district in Shinjuku.)

tekitō/ 適当 This can have a positive meaning (as in easy-going) or a negative one (half-assed) A typical use of this word is something like "He likes going with the flow, so he probably hasn't made any plans yet." (**Kare-wa tekitō dakara, tabun mada yotei tatete nai-yo.**/ 彼は適当だから、多分まだ予定立ててないよ。)

kao-ga hiroi/ 顔が広い literally means someone with a wide face. It's an expression for someone who is a social butterfly, someone who has lots of connections and/or friends.

nīto/ ニート a young adult who is neither working nor going to school.

mai pēsu/ マイペース This is based on the English phrase "my pace." You can use it to describe yourself or anyone who does things at their own pace.

ike-men/ イケメン a good-looking young man.

ike-dan/ イケダン a husband who's both good-looking and hard-working, a good husband/father, (or good husband/father material).

kakkoii/ かっこいい cool, handsome.

oyaji/ オヤジ This is sort of like using Pop, Grandpa or Gramps to refer to an older man in a rude way.

charai/ チャラい slang term used to describe a guy as frivolous, not someone you take seriously.

fushigi-chan/ 不思議ちゃん a strange, dreamy type of girl.

kawaii/ かわいい cute, pretty. This is probably the most overused adjective among females aged between three and 80 years old. You'll hear it a lot more often than you'll want to.

kirei-me/ きれいめ : **kirei** = pretty/clean. **kirei-me** refers to a man or woman who is attractive in a clean-cut, well-kept kind of way.

ukeru/ ウケる a word used to respond to something funny said by someone else ("How funny!", or "That's funny!").

norokeru/ のろける to go on about one's own boyfriend/girlfriend/new love interest with pride and giddiness. To be smitten and unable to shut up about it.

hitomishiri/ 人見知り to be shy (on first meeting).

nanpa/ ナンパ to pick up someone, usually guys picking up girls.

gyaku-nan/ 逆ナン (a girl) picking up a guy.

tenparu/ テンパる to freak out, be overwhelmed

gyaku-gire/ 逆ギレ This means to reverse a situation, specifically used when a person who should be the one asking for forgiveness is turning the situation around on the "injured" party and getting upset instead.

THE INFAMOUS F-WORD

This the first swear word anyone learns, and we'll show you more uses for it in *Curses and Insults*. It's also the most versatile word in the English language. It can be used any way you like: insert it in between any word, sentence, letter—it probably fits. Its street value is high enough that we thought we'd share some of its uses here.

1. v. to have sex (e.g.: I like to fuck/ **yaru-no-ga suki**/ ヤルのが好き) ***(ヤル literally means "do it.")

2. n. the act of having sex (e.g.: That was a good fuck/ **(fakku-ga) yokkatta**/（ファックが）良かった ***(usually the F-word is implied).

3. adj. can be used to modify any word for more passion. Very, extremely. (e.g.: that was a fucking amazing piece of pie, Mrs. Smith!/ **Sumisu-san, sugoku oishii pai deshita-yo!**/ スミスさん、すごく美味しいパイでしたよ !)

4. to not care (e.g.: I don't give a fuck/ **dō-demo ii**/ どうでもいい)

5. to disregard, ignore (used with -it, -that) (e.g.: Fuck it/ **kuso kurae!**/ くそ食らえ !)

6. to mess up, destroy, mangle, etc. (used with suffix -up) (e.g.: I heard he fucked up his teeth/ **kare-wa ha-o mecha-kucha-ni shichatta rashii-yo**/ 彼は歯をめちゃくちゃにしちゃったらしいよ)

7. an exclamation of emotion, can be happy or angry (e.g.: Oh fuck!/ **uwatt!**/ うわっ !)

8. a general insult (e.g.: Fuck you/ **shine**/ 死ね)

A FEW OTHER THINGS YOU SHOULD KNOW

The Japanese street scene is full of characters. Sometimes it seems that everyone you see is in costume. Half the girls you see look like they're in a girl band and the other half look like Bo-peep. Guys look like they've walked straight off the manga page or anime screen. Archetypes are everywhere. Here are just a few of the types you might run into. Don't worry, it's all perfectly normal; it's even fun!

Otaku (オタク)

Basically, the equivalent of a geek in the US. This is someone with an intense obsession with / focus on some subject or other, often to the exclusion of other things. As a result, they can often relate only to other **otaku** who share an identical obsession. **Otakus** are usually deep into computers/technology, video games, manga or anime, or just can't get enough net-surfing, but there are plenty of other obsessive interests that can get someone classified as an **otaku**.

Maid Cafes/**meido kafe**/ メイドカフェ

Akihabara is a Tokyo neighborhood that's a mecca for electronics, very appealing to **otakus**. It's also famous for the phenomenon known as Maid Cafes (which are also appealing to **otakus**, as a way of being out in the world without having to be in the real world). In the early 2000s maid cafes started getting a lot of media attention and their popularity snowballed. Soon, they were recognized as a legitimate subculture. Basically, how it works is this: you go to a maid cafe, you are greeted by cute Japanese girls in maid costumes with a "welcome home, master!," you sit down at your table, order expensive coffee and dessert, and enjoy the sweet and, perhaps, rejuvenating qualities of your hostess. Many men (and women, at ギャルソン喫茶／**gyaruson kissa**/a coffeehouse with characters from Yaoi (boys love) manga and anime) frequent these establishments for a few reasons. First, they are anime fans, or, more specifically, fans of the "maid character". Second, they like being fawned over by beautiful girls. One might "**moe~~!**" over these girls. ("萌えー！"—in this case as a verb, is to feel an obsessive, deep infatuation with the said object, usually a particular character from an anime, movie, or manga, in this case, a maid at a maid cafe. It is close to "arousal", but not always. It is a fiery, passionate feeling felt uniquely towards one object or person).

Cosplay/**kosupure**/コスプレ originally a Japanglish term, has now been re-introduced into the Western mainstream as another fascinating subculture from the Land of the Rising Sun. Once an **otaku** subculture, cosplay is now a part of the **otaku** mainstream. Costume Play ("cosplay" for short), consists of dressing up as a character (fictional, nonfiction, female, male, monsters, professions, basically whatever) and taking on their persona, usually for a limited amount of time (at an cosplay event, for example). There are cosplay events held in Japan throughout the year for those wanting to dress up as their favorite anime character, or just to hang out and take in the spectacles. These events are no longer limited to Japan; they're held everywhere from Hong Kong to Italy to the U.S. These

days, cosplay can be seen in **kosupure izakaya** ／コ
スプレ居酒屋 (theme restaurants/bars) such as Maid
Cafes. So if one ever gets the urge to be in the com-
pany of a cute girl dressed up as a flight attendant,
they need not go any further than Akihabara to make
their desires a reality.

Lolita/**rorīta**/ロリータ A fashion style within a subculture that has been around since the 70s but has
been gaining in popularity and mainstream aware-
ness since the early 00s. The style is characterized
by frilly clothes laden with ribbons and lace and is
influenced by different historical periods, for example,
the Rococo-Era in France. Lolita is a good example of
the "Japanizification" of the West. Innocence, youth
and cuteness are desirable, and this style accentuates
them. Different style elements have been combined
with the full skirts and frills to create different sub-
styles, like the Goth Lolita (macabre jewelry and color
schemes), Punk Lolita, and others. Colors "Lolitas" wear
include: white, black, red, pink, blue (think Alice in
Wonderland) and, in the fall, brown and purple. It is a
fashion trend that ignores mainstream popular trends
or styles deemed "attractive" to men (assuming these
girls are heterosexual), but instead are worn for the
wearer's pleasure. Some girls choose to dress like this
24/7, others, considered "weekenders", "dress up" only
on their days off. "Lolita" as a cultural phenomenon
has been fueled by and brought to the attention of
mainstream media thanks to films like *Shimotsuma
Story* (下妻物語) written by Nobara Takemoto (嶽本

野ばら), a famous and emblematic literary figure within the subculture.

Girl Bands

Contributing to the innocence-as-sexy concept are the girl bands of J-Pop (Japanese pop). AKB48 is one of the many girl bands that have been in and out of fashion over the years. A product of the Akihabara subculture, it started out as a performance group and pranced its way into the mainstream. Another all-girl "super band" (one of the first) is Morning Musime (**Mōningu Musume**/ モーニング娘。 or **Mo-Musu**/ モー娘。 for short). These girl bands are characterized by young, innocent-looking, cute Japanese girls who can dance and sing mediocrely. Member turnover rate is very high and the girls are essentially recyclable. Japan is full of girl bands like this one, and similar bands coming out of Korea have lately been infiltrating the Japanese media. Like J-Pop bands, K-Pop girl bands consist of four or more girls, but are sexier and more hip-hop-influenced than their Japanese counterparts.

Vijuaru-kei (bui-kei)/ ヴィジュアル系 (V 系)

These are rock musicians characterized by a feminine-leaning appearance, heavy stage make-up, and outlandish and goth-inspired hair and clothing. **Vijuaru-kei** bands are musically influenced by various genres, including but not limited to: hard rock, heavy metal, goth, new-romantic and punk.

Have I seen you before?
Mae-ni atta-koto nai?

Do you want to sit down?
Suwaranai?

Did you two come here by yourselves?
Futari-de kiteru-no?

Do you know this song?
Kono kyoku shitteru?

I know it.
Shitteru.

Is someone sitting here?
Koko dare-ka suwatteru?

You need to drink more.
Motto nomina-yo.

Haven't you drunk too much?
Nomisugi-janai?

You're a good dancer.
Dansu umai-ne.

I have a good idea.
Ii koto kangaeta.

Shall we leave?
Denai?

May I have your phone number?
Denwa bangō oshiete-kureru?

Do you have something to write with?
Nan-ka kaku-mono aru?

9

Chit Chat

Are you having a good time?

Tanoshinderu?
楽しんでる?

If someone says **Tanoshinderu?** to you, the best answer is **Un** or **Mane**, meaning "Yeah, I am."

You look like you're having a good time.

◆ Tanoshisō-dane.
楽しそうだね。

Yeah, I'm having fun.

Tanoshii-yo.
楽しいよ。

No, not really.

Mā, sō-ne.
まあ、そうね。

Anmari.
あんまり。

Betsu-ni.
別に。

Mā, sō-ne can indicate either (indifferent) agreement or subtle disagreement (subtle being the best disagreement in this situation!) depending on how you say it. Saying it with a lack of enthusiasm, or the latter two, will show that you're not really enjoying yourself. And of course this hints that you'd rather move on or go home!

We're having a good time, aren't we?	Tanoshii-nē? 楽しいねえ?
Did you two come here by yourselves?	Futari-de kiteru-no? 二人で来てるの?

If more than two people, replace **futari** with **san-nin** 三人 (three), **yo-nin** 四人 (four) etc.

Shall we drink together?	Issho-ni nomanai? 一緒に飲まない?

"Shall we drink together?" doesn't quite make the top 100 list of all-time great pick-up lines, but nonetheless, it's very effective in Japan. If the mood is right and someone is eyeballing you, this is a good one to get the party going (or at least to sit at their table).

Excuse me.	Sumimasen. すみません。
Has someone reserved this seat?	Kono-seki aiteru? この席空いてる?

This is a clever way to say "May I sit here?"

Is someone sitting here?	**Koko dare-ka suwatteru?** ここ誰か座ってる?
Do you want to sit down?	**Suwaranai?** 座らない?
May I sit down?	**Suwatte-mo-ii?** 座ってもいい?
Let me sit down.	**Suwarasete.** 座らせて。
Shuffle over/ Make room.	**Tsumete.** つめて。 **Chotto ii?** ちょっといい?

Chotto ii? literally means "Excuse me, okay?" You should point or look at the seat to make yourself clear.

What did you say?	**Nante itta-no?** 何て言ったの? **Nani?** 何? **E?** え? **Nante ittan-dayo?** ♂ 何て言ったんだよ?

Nante ittan-dayo? is quite accusative, and is not to be used in a delicate situation, or when you're trying to make friends!

Do you come here often?

Yoku koko kuru-no?
よくここ来るの？

Have I seen you before?

Mae-ni atta-koto nai?
前に会ったことない？

Your English is good.

Eigo umai-ne.
英語うまいね。

While introducing yourself to a Japanese, you could try getting them to speak a bit in English, and ingratiate yourself with this and the other phrases in *Say What?* Even if the conversation continues in Japanese, you'll have kicked off on the right foot!

What music do you like?

Don'na ongaku-ga suki?
どんな音楽が好き？

Whose kind of music do you like?

Dare-no ongaku-ga suki?
誰の音楽が好き？

Do you know this song?

Kono uta/kyoku shitteru?
この歌／曲知ってる？

I know it.

Shitteru.
知ってる。

Shitteru-yo.
知ってるよ。

I don't know it.

Shiranai.
知らない。

Shiran. ♂
知らん。

Shall we dance?

Odoranai?
踊らない？

I don't feel like dancing yet.

Mada odoru-ki shinai.
まだ踊る気しない。

Mada odoranai.
まだ踊らない。

You're a good dancer.

Dansu umai-ne.
ダンスうまいね。

How do you know of this place?

Nan-de koko shitten-no?
何でここ知ってんの？

I heard from my friends.

Tomodachi-ni kiita.
友達に聞いた。

Tomodachi-ni kiitan-da. ♂
友達に聞いたんだ。

Where else do you go to dance?

Hoka-ni don'na kurabu-ni iku-no?
他にどんなクラブに行くの？

How long have you been in Japan?

Dono-gurai Nihon-ni iru-no?
どのぐらい日本にいるの？

Do you like Japanese girls/boys?

Nihon-no on'na-no-ko/otoko-no-ko suki?
日本の女の子／男の子好き？

Let's party!

Tanoshimō-yo!
楽しもうよ！

Let's get drunk!

Konya-wa nomō!
今夜は飲もう！

Yopparaō!
酔っ払おう！

Moriagarō!
盛りあがろう！

What are you drinking?

Nani nonden-no?
何飲んでんの？

Have you been drinking a lot?

Kanari nonderu?
かなり飲んでる？

Well, drink some more.

Jā, motto nomeba!
じゃあ、もっと飲めば！

You need to drink more.

Motto nomina-yo!
もっと飲みなよ！

You can handle your drink, can't you?

Osake tsuyoi-ne.
お酒強いね。

Are you drunk?

Yotteru?
酔ってる？

Haven't you drunk too much?

Nomisugi-janai?
飲み過ぎじゃない？

Maybe you should stop drinking.	**Mō nomu-no yametara.** もう飲むの止めたら。
Are you okay?	**Daijōbu?** 大丈夫?
You're kind.	**Yasashii-ne.** 優しいね。
What time did you come here?	**Nanji-goro kita-no?** 何時ごろ来たの?
What time are you leaving?	**Nanji-goro kaeru-no?** 何時ごろ帰るの?
I haven't decided.	**Kimetenai.** 決めてない。
If I have a good time, I'll stay.	**Tanoshikattara iru.** 楽しかったらいる。
If this gets boring, I'll go (home).	**Tsumanakattara kaeru.** つまんなかったら帰る。
I'll help you to have a good time.	**Issho-ni tanoshimō-yo.** 一緒に楽しもうよ。
This is boring!	**Omoshiroku-nai!** 面白くない! **Tsuman'nai!** つまんない! **Tsuman'nē! ♂** つまんねえ!

The latter two, if said slowly, are clever ways to say "What you said isn't funny!" or "Your joke is stupid!" They are also adjectives with certain nouns: **Tsuman'nai yatsu!** つまんないやつ! You're boring! or He/she's boring! **Tsuman'nē eiga** つまんねえ映画 This is a boring movie etc.

Shall we go somewhere else?	Dokka ikanai? どっか行かない?
Shall we leave?	Denai? 出ない?
Can my friends come?	Tomodachi-mo issho-de ii? 友達も一緒でいい?
I'd like to stay here longer.	Mada koko-ni itai. まだздеここにいたい。
What's next?	Kono ato dō-suru-no? この後どうするの?
Have you decided?	Kimatta? 決まった?
I haven't decided yet.	Mada kimetenai. まだ決めてない。
It's up to you.	Makaseru. 任せる。 Makaseru-yo. 任せるよ。

Anything's fine.

Nan-demo ii.
何でもいい。

Nan-demo ii-yo.
何でもいいよ。

Either will do.

Dotchi-demo ii.
どっちでもいい。

Dotchi-demo ii-yo.
どっちでもいいよ。

I have a good idea.

Ii kangae-ga aru.
いい考えがある。

Ii-koto kangaeta.
いい事考えた。

How does that sound?

Sore-de ii?
それでいい？

Dō?
どう？

Good idea.

Guddo aidia!
グッド・アイディア！

You've got your head on straight today, haven't you?

Kyō saeteru-nē?
今日さえてるねえ？

I've got my head on straight today.

Kyō saeteru.
今日さえてる。

Anywhere's okay.	Doko-demo ii. どこでもいい。 Doko-demo ii-yo. どこでもいいよ。
I'll take you home.	Okutteku-yo. 送ってくよ。 Okutte iku-yo. 送って行くよ。
I wanna know more about you.	Anata-no-koto motto shiritai. ♀ あなたの事もっと知りたい。 Kimi-no-koto motto shiritai. ♂ 君の事もっと知りたい。
We think the same way, don't we?	Ki-ga au-nē? 気が合うねえ?
Shall we meet again?	Mata aeru? また会える?
When can I see you next time?	Kondo itsu aeru? 今度いつ会える?
May I call you?	Denwa shite-mo ii? 電話してもいい?
May I have your phone number?	Denwa bangō oshiete-kureru? 電話番号教えてくれる?

Do you have something to write with?

Nan-ka kaku-mono aru?
何か書く物ある?

I enjoyed myself.

Tanoshikatta.
楽しかった。

Thank you.

Arigatō.
ありがとう。

Take care.

Ki-o-tsukete-ne.
気を付けてね。

See you later.

Jā mata-ne.
じゃあまたね。

Mata-ne.
またね。

Jā-ne.
じゃあね。

See you tomorrow.

Jā mata ashita-ne.
じゃあまた明日ね。

Mata ashita-ne.
また明日ね。

Jā ashita-ne.
じゃあ明日ね。

Bye (bye)!

Bai-bāi!
バイバーイ!

I'll show you.
Misete ageru.

Look at that!
Are mite!

Don't look!
Miruna-yo!

Let's go shopping in Shibuya.
Shibuya-de shoppingu shiyō.

I don't want to see.
Mitaku-nai.

Do you know a good place?
Ii tokoro aru?

I know a good place.
Aru(-yo).

Let's go to your favorite club.
Anata-no yoku iku kurabu-ni ikō.

Shall we go clubbing this Friday?
Kinyōbi kurabu-ni ikō-ka?

10

Check It Out!

Look!	Mite! 見て！
Look at this!	Kore mite! これ見て！
Look at that!	Are mite! あれ見て！
Take a look.	Chotto mite. ちょっと見て。
Don't look!	Minai-de! 見ないで！ Miruna-yo! ♂ 見るなよ！
I'll show you.	Misete ageru. 見せてあげる。

Miseru.
見せる。

I won't show you.　　**Misete agenai.**
見せてあげない。

Misenai.
見せない。

Did you see (it)?　　**Mita?**
見た？

I saw (it).　　**Mita-mita.**
見た見た。

This is a (usually feminine) emphatic form, which normally shows enthusiasm.

Mita.
見た。

Mita-yo.
見たよ。

I didn't see (it).　　**Minakatta.**
見なかった。

I couldn't see (it).　　**Mienakatta.**
見えなかった。

When you can't see something because something else is in the way.

Mirenakatta.
見れなかった。

When you can't see something because of your own lack of vision or perception.

I don't want to see (it).	Mitaku-nai. 見たくない。

Do you want to see...?	...Mitai? …見たい？

Shall we go and see it?	Mite miyō-ka? 見てみようか？

This is of course a good phrase when thinking about movies. The movies in Japan are quite expensive, and with most theaters downtown, are not such a popular option for people in the suburbs. With the proliferation of home theater systems, many people now borrow videos or DVDs instead.

Shall we get a video/ DVD (instead)?	(Sono kawari) Bideo/DVD -o karite miyō-ka? (その代わり)ビデオ／DVDを 借りてみようか？

There are plenty of other socializing options though, with perhaps the most common being shopping, karaoke and going drinking or clubbing.

Shall we go shopping?	Shoppingu shi-ni ikō-ka? ショッピングしに行こうか？

Let's go (shopping in) Shibuya.	Shibuya-de shoppingu shiyō. 渋谷でショッピングしよう。

I want to go shopping for clothes.   Yōfuku-o kaitai.
洋服を買いたい。

In Japan, you usually go social shopping downtown, in the big (and attractive, especially to women!) department stores (such as Ginza in Tokyo and Umeda in Osaka) and specialty shopping districts (e.g. Tokyo's Akihabara is famed for its electronics shops). Suburban malls, which are not nearly as big as in the US, are for more mundane clothes or food shopping. A casual evening or night out in Japan will often involve karaoke.

Do you like karaoke?   Karaoke suki?
カラオケ好き？

Let's sing karaoke.   Karaoke utaō/ikō.
カラオケ歌おう／行こう。

Karaoke literally means "without orchestra." You usually sing in karaoke "boxes" dotted around cities but especially in major railway stations and entertainment areas. The "boxes" are collections of many rooms, where you can sing, eat and drink in relative privacy. The singing itself consists of individuals/pairs/groups singing the vocals of their favorite songs, backed by digitised instruments. Like all their fun, Japanese take this very seriously. You can get drinks in karaoke bars, but many places are dedicated to alcohol.

Shall we go bowling?	Bōringu-ni ikō-ka? ボーリングに行こうか?
Shall we go to the game center/arcade?	Gēmu sentā-ni ikō-ka? ゲームセンターに行こうか?

Game centers are common in Japan and are where kids can go and play video-games, air-hockey, do "print clubs" **purikura** プリクラ (taking photos of yourself and making funny stickers out of them). They are big, noisy and fun places. But older kids might prefer the following options.

Shall we go (for a drink) drinking?	(Chotto) Nomi-ni ikō-ka? (ちょっと)飲みに行こうか?
I wonder where we should go.	Doko-ga ii kanā. どこがいいかなあ。
Do you know a good place (near here)?	(Kono hen-ni) ii tokoro aru? (この辺に)いい所ある?
I know a good place.	Aru(-yo). ある(よ)。

Drinking is a vital social activity in Japan, where the inhibitions of the day can be partially cast aside in a friendlier environment than the workplace. "After-work" drinks are usually at a local **izakaya** 居酒屋, or, in summer, an outdoor beer hall. Small **izakayas** are numerous, and they provide good food as well as plenty of beer, whisky (or whatever!) They are often quite "Japanese-y" inside, with low tables to sit at, encouraging close conversation and a lively atmosphere. There are more and more Western-style bars these days, but they're mainly in downtown entertainment areas. Two things to expect at most **izakayas** are table charges, known as **otoshi**, which are small dishes that are served before your drink orders are taken, whether you like it or not, and you are charged for it (anywhere between 300-500 yen). Also, **nomihōdai**, or all-you-can-drink, are becoming more common at most of these establishments. These can be fun or dangerous.

Serious nights out involve going downtown, to night-club districts like Roppongi and Kabukichō in Tokyo and Minami and Shinsaibashi in Osaka, where there are incredible arrays of bars, clubs and parlors catering to (literally) every taste. But because the trains and buses don't run from about midnight to 6 a.m., if you don't live nearby or have lots of money for a taxi, it pays to plan ahead!

Shall we go clubbing this Friday/Saturday?	Kinyōbi/Doyōbi kurabu-ni ikō-ka? 金曜日／土曜日クラブに行こうか？
What sort of club should we go to?	Don'na kurabu-ga ii? どんなクラブがいい？
Let's go to your favorite club.	Anata-no yoku iku kurabu-ni ikō. ♀ あなたのよく行くクラブに行こう。 Kimi-no yoku iku kurabu-ni ikō-yō. ♂ 君のよく行くクラブに行こうよ。

Use **yoku iku** to indicate a place you go to often.

11

Curses and Insults

The next two chapters are full of words to use when you're ready to get stuck into someone and tell them what you think! This chapter is general insults and tough talk that you can throw into conversations to add a bit of punch, and the next, *Fighting Words*, is about some nasty situations you could end up in while in Japan—and ways out of them!

There are two things to bear in mind when ripping into someone with phrases like these. First, make sure they were insulting or trying to harm you! Sometimes the Japanese pay compliments in seemingly strange and roundabout ways. And secondly, if you do decide to unleash, make sure your attitude matches the words. Remember what we said about how you say things being as important as what you say? A forceful phrase said softly just sounds silly, but a punchy phrase backed with menace is frightening.

Damn it!　　　　　　　Chikushō!
　　　　　　　　　　　　ちくしょう!

Usually said to yourself.

Shit!　　　　　　　　Kuso!
　　　　　　　　　　　　くそ!

Meaning "feces," **Kuso!** can be said to yourself, just as Westerners say "Shit!"

Shit, I fucked up!　　Ikkenai! ♀
Oh, shit!　　　　　　いっけない!

　　　　　　　　　　　　Ikkene! ♂
　　　　　　　　　　　　いっけね!

Literally means "It's not good!" Usually said to yourself.

What do you want?!　Nani-yo?! ♀
　　　　　　　　　　　　何よ?!

　　　　　　　　　　　　Nanda-yo?! ♂
　　　　　　　　　　　　何だよ?!

　　　　　　　　　　　　Nan-ka monku aru-no?!
　　　　　　　　　　　　何か文句あるの?!

These are basic, all-round good phrases to use when someone really pisses you off. They usually command respect, or at least let you establish yourself.

What did you say?　　Nante itta-no?
　　　　　　　　　　　　何て言ったの?

　　　　　　　　　　　　Nante ittan-dayo? ♂
　　　　　　　　　　　　何て言ったんだよ?

Who do you think you're talking to?	Dare-ni mukatte itten-dayo? ♂ 誰に向かって言ってんだよ？
Why do you talk like that?!	Nan-de son'na-koto iu-no?! 何でそんな事言うの？！ Nan-de son'na-koto iun-dayo?! 何でそんな事言うんだよ？！

If you're positive a Japanese person is talking derogatorily about you, these phrases are good to use. But be careful sometimes the Japanese are complimenting you!

Are you stupid, or what?	Baka-janai? ばかじゃない？

This phrase is a superb example of the importance of pronunciation. To mean "Are you stupid, or what?" you must use a rising intonation (making it a rhetorical question). With a flat or falling intonation it means the opposite, "I'm/You're no fool!"

You're stupid!	**Baka!** ばか！ **Baka-yarō!** ♂ ばかやろう！
You look stupid! **That's stupid!**	**Baka-mitai!** ばかみたい！ **Baka-jan!** ばかじゃん！

-**Jan** is a colloquial suffix which means the same as -**deshō?/-darō?** ーでしょう？ ーだろう？ or -**yonē?** ーよねえ？, i.e. asking the other person to confirm your opinion. Only people under the age of about 35 use -**jan**. じゃん is used in the Yokohama area.

What you did was stupid!	**Baka-da!** ばかだ！
You're crazy!	**Ikareten-janai-no!** いかれてんじゃないの！ **Kichigai!** 気違い！
Stop acting stupid/ **Don't joke around** **with me!**	**Fuzakenai-deyo!** ♀ ふざけないでよ！ **Fuzakeruna-yo!** ♂ ふざけるなよ！

Used in cases where someone is acting stupidly or has said something stupid.

Fuzaken-ja nēyo! ♀
ふざけんじゃねえよ!

This is especially used when someone is being cheeky or has underestimated the speaker's power or status.

Don't act stupid/ **Stop acting stupid!**	**Baka yamete-yo!** ♀ ばか止めてよ!
	Baka yamero-yo! ♂ ばか止めろよ!
	Baka yamena-yo! ♀ ばか止めなよ!
	Baka yatten-ja nēyo! ♂ ばかやってんじゃねえよ!

These phrases can all be used when someone pisses you off. Phrases beginning with **baka** ("stupid," "crazy") can also be voiced with concern for a friend's silly, irrational behavior.

Don't say (such) **stupid things!**	**Baka iwanai-deyo!** ♀ ばか言わないでよ!
	Baka itten'na-yo! ♂ ばか言ってんなよ!
	Neten'na-yo! ♂ 寝てんなよ!

Neten'na-yo! literally means "Wake up!"

Liar!	**Usotsuki!** 嘘つき!

You've got a big mouth!	**Oshaberi!** おしゃべり!

Someone who's always spreading the latest rumor, people's secrets, etc.

Get your head out of your ass!	Neboken-ja nēyo! ♂ 寝ぼけんじゃねえよ！

Literally means "Aren't you half-asleep (because of what you did/are doing)?" Depending upon your tone of voice, this phrase can be very funny or very harsh.

That's a lie!	Son'na-no uso-da! そんなの嘘だ！
	Son'na-no uso-dayo! そんなの嘘だよ！
	Uso bakkari! 嘘ばっかり！
Don't lie!	Uso tsukanai-deyo! ♀ 嘘つかないでよ！
	Uso tsukuna-yo! ♂ 嘘つくなよ！
Stop it!	Yamete-yo! ♀ 止めてよ！
	Yamero-yo! ♂ 止めろよ！
You shouldn't do that/ Don't do that!	Dame! だめ！
	Dame-dayo! ♂ だめだよ！

Why do you do things like that?	Nan-de son'na-koto suru-no? 何でそんな事するの？
Why did you do such a thing?	Nan-de son'na-koto shita-no? 何でそんな事したの？
Leave him/her alone!	Hottoite-agete! ♀ ほっといてあげて！ Hottoite-yare-yo! ♂ ほっといてやれよ！ Hottoke-yo! ♂ ほっとけよ！
Do as I say!	Itta-tōri-ni shite! ♀ 言った通りにして！ Itta-tōri-ni shiro-yo! ♂ 言った通りにしろよ！

This is the limit!	Ii kagen-ni shite-yo! いいかげんにしてよ! Ii kagen-ni shiro-yo! ♂ いいかげんにしろよ!
Stop it! You're being persistent/annoying!	Shitsukoi! しつこい!

When someone is being persistent.

Give it back!	Kaeshite-yo! 返してよ! Kaeshite-kure! ♂ 返してくれ! Kaese-yo! ♂ 返せよ!
Leave me alone!	Hottoite-yo! ♀ ほっといてよ! Hottoite-kure-yo! ♂ ほっといてくれよ!
Leave us alone!	Atashi-tachi dake-ni shite-yo! ♀ あたし達だけにしてよ! Boku-tachi dake-ni shite-kure-yo! ♂ 僕達だけにしてくれよ!
Get out of here/ Fuck off!	Kiero! 消えろ! Mukō itte-yo! ♀ 向こう行ってよ!

Atchi itte-yo! ♀
あっち行ってよ！

Atchi ike-yo! ♂
あっち行けよ！

Dokka itchimae! ♂
どっか行っちまえ！

Dokka itte-yo! ♀
どっか行ってよ！

Dokka ike-yo! ♂
どっか行けよ！

Hayaku inakunare-yo! ♂
早くいなくなれよ！

Urochoro shiten'na! ♂
うろちょろしてんな！

Totto-to usero! ♂
とっととうせろ！

Come here!

Chotto kotchi kite! ♀
ちょっとこっち来て！

Kotchi oide-yo! ♀ (b→g)
こっちおいでよ！

Kotchi koi-yo! ♂
こっち来いよ！

You're noisy!

Urusai!
うるさい！

Urusē-na! ♂
うるせえな！

Urusē-yo! ♂
うるせえよ！

Urusēn-dayo! ♂
うるせえんだよ！

Shut up!	**Damatte-yo!** ♀
	黙ってよ!
	Damare-yo! ♂
	黙れよ!
Stop your babbling!	**Gocha-gocha/Gata-gata itten-ja nēyo!** ♂
	ごちゃごちゃ／がたがた言ってんじゃねえよ!
Be quiet!	**Shizuka-ni shite-yo!** ♀ (b→g)
	静かにしてよ!
	Shizuka-ni shiro-yo! ♂
	静かにしろよ!

Both phrases can be used playfully between boyfriend and girlfriend. In a movie theater, pub, etc., you should first say **Shizuka-ni shite kudasai** 静かにしてくだ下さい。 If there are no results, **Shizuka-ni shite-yo!** or **Shizuka-ni shiro-yo!** should do the trick. Still no progress? Throw in a couple of **Urusen-dayo!**'s.

You asshole!	**Kono kusottare!** ♂
	このくそったれ!

Literally means "You have shit around your asshole!"

Bitch	**Bitchi**
	ビッチ
	Ama
	あま
	Iya-na on'na
	嫌な女

Sissy   **Memeshii**
                             女々しい

Slut   **Shiri-garu on'na**
                             尻軽女

You bitch!   **Kono kuso-on'na!** ♂
                             (b/g→g)
                             このくそ女！

You whore!   **Yariman!** (b/g→g)
                             ヤリまん！

                             Kōshū-benjyo! (→g)
                             公衆便所！

This means a girl who will go to bed with anyone. 公衆便所 literally means "public restroom".

Cunt!   **Kant!**
                             カント!

Loser!   **Dasai!**
                             ダサい！

Creepy!   **Kimoi!**
                             キモイ！

This guy is a creep!   **Koitsu kimoi!**
                             こいつキモイ！

You're saying they are unfashionable, or that their talk is uncool.

Shorty!	**Chibi!** ちび!
	Gaki! がき!
Short legs!	**Tansoku!** 短足!
Weakling/Pussy!	**Yowa-mushi!** (→b) 弱虫!
You ain't got balls!	**Konjō-nashi!** 根性なし!

Means you're lacking in the "brave" department.

Chinchin chiisai! ♂
ちんちん小さい!

This literally means "You have a small penis!" As you'd expect, this is a very serious insult!

You're ugly!	**Busu!** (ugly girl) (b/g→g) ぶす!
	Busaiku! (both) 不細工!

Busaiku! is the worst word to say to a girl.

You pig!	**Buta!** 豚!
	Debu! でぶ!

Said to girls and to obese boys.

Fag!   Okama!
                              おかま！

Said to a boy who acts or dresses in a feminine manner.

Tomboy!   Otoko-on'na!
                              <ruby>男<rt>おとこ</rt></ruby> <ruby>女<rt>おんな</rt></ruby>！

                              Otenba!
                              おてんば！

This is an uncommon insult in Japan.

White boy!   Haku-jin!
                              <ruby>白人<rt>はくじん</rt></ruby>！

You're the lowest!   Saitei!
                              <ruby>最低<rt>さいてい</rt></ruby>！

                              Saitei-dayo!
                              <ruby>最低<rt>さいてい</rt></ruby>だよ！

You're narrow-minded.   Kokoro(-ga) semai-yo-nē.
心(が)狭いよねえ。

Don't be so cocky!   Erasō-ni suruna-yo!
偉そうにするなよ!

You're a tightwad!   Kechi!
けち!
Do-kechi!
どけち!

Do-kechi is even tighter than **kechi**, which is already a strong word.

You're a dirtbag!   Kitanai!
汚い!

Don't fuck with me!   Namen-ja nēyo! ♂
なめんじゃねえよ!

This literally means "Don't lick me!" If someone says **Nanda-yo?** 何だよ? to you, you could just say one of the above and walk away (as the winner). But the Japanese themselves don't use this that much. Less direct insults can have more effect.

If you don't have time to "socialize," just fire off one or two of these parting shots:

What a nasty person!   Yana-yatsu! ♀
嫌なやつ!

What a geek!   Hen-na-yatsu! ♂
変なやつ！

What a chump!   Hen-na-yarō! ♂
変な野郎！

Fuck you!/Go to hell!   Kutabare! ♂
くたばれ！

Shine! ♂
死ね！

Don't try to be cool!   Kakko tsuken'na-yo! ♂
かっこつけんなよ！

Let's finish this now!   Keri-o tsuke-yōze! ♂
けりをつけようぜ！

I'm going to kick your ass!   Bukkoroshite-yaru! ♂
ぶっ殺してやる！

Korosu-zo! ♂
殺すぞ！

These literally mean "I'm going to hit you till you die!" and "I'm going to kill you!" They're harsh phrases—expect to throw a few punches after you say them!

You fucker!   Kono-yarō! ♂
You little shit!   この野郎！

Serious fighting words! Usually said before or while the right hook is connecting.

That hurts!	Itai! 痛い！ Itē-na! ♂ 痛えな！

These phrases are said to ensure the offender knows you're hurt. **Itai** is said when you've been made to hurt yourself.

You little rat! **(Check this geek out!)**	Nani koitsu! 何こいつ！

Said about anyone doing anything, but usually not to their face.

Who do you think **you are?!**	Nani-sama-no tsumori?! ♀ 何様のつもり？！ Anta nani-sama na-no?! ♀ あんた何様なの？！ Nani temē?! ♂ 何てめえ？！

Anta is a shorter way for girls to say **anata** "you," and in the Kanto area, **anta** is considered to be harsher than **anata**. The first two phrases are mockingly disrespectful, and **temē** is a bad boy's word for "you." **Nani temē?!** can be said to their face—with care!

The following insults don't have exact equivalents in English, and a few of these are negative adjectives rather than insults, but they're used a lot in Japan.

ketsu-no-ana ga chiisai/ ケツの穴が小さい /literally someone with a small anus, this term is used for someone who's unforgiving, close-minded, or just a jerk.

men-kui/ 面食い /literally means someone who eats another person's face, It's used to describe someone who only likes or dates good-looking people.

nechi-nechi shiteru/ ねちねちしてる /an onomatopoeic word for being nit-picky.

omae-no kā-chan debeso!/ おまえの母ちゃんデベソ！/ "Your mom has an out-ie!" Kind of childish and not used in real fights, but is well-known and can be used humorously.

12

Fighting Words

Have you ever noticed that while you're waiting in line for something—it doesn't matter what—for some reason people seem to think their position is at the front of the line? The following phrases should get your point across.

We're making a line.	**Naranderun-dakedo.** 並んでるんだけど。
Don't push!	**Osanai-deyo!** ♀ 押さないでよ!
	Osuna-yo! ♂ 押すなよ!
What's this old man doing?!	**Nani kono jiji'i?!** 何このジジイ?!
	Nanda-yo kono jiji'i?! 何だよこのジジイ?!

Jiji'i is from (the much politer form) **ojii-san** (grandfather/old man).

What's this old woman doing?!	Nani kono babā?! 何このババア？！
	Nanda-yo kono babā?! 何だよこのババア？！

Babā is from (the again much politer form) **obā-san** (grandmother/old woman).

Man, they're slow!	Osoi-nē! 遅いねえ!
	Osoi-nā! ♂ 遅いなあ!
Could you go a bit faster?	Mō chotto hayaku...? もうちょっと速く？
The service here is bad.	Koko-no sābisu-wa yoku-nai. ここのサービスはよくない。
Do you want to say something?!	Nan-ka-iitai-no?! 何か言いたいの？！

The Japanese are infamous for staring, especially at things foreign or unusual. To have them return to their own affairs, a simple **Nanda-yo?!** 何だよ？！ or **Nan-ka yō?!** 何か用？！ works well. But then again, the Japanese are also known for their persistence. If these two fail, simply tell them:

Don't look at me!	(Kotchi) minai-deyo! ♀ (こっち)見ないでよ！
	(Kotchi) miruna-yo! ♂ (こっち)見るなよ！

Miten-ja nēyo! ♂
見てんじゃねえよ！

Don't stare at me!   **Jiro-jiro minai-deyo!** ♀
ジロジロ見ないでよ！

Jiro-jiro miruna-yo! ♂
ジロジロ見るなよ！

These phrases can be used in most situations to get your point across forcefully.

Gan tobashiten-ja nēyo! ♂
ガンとばしてんじゃねえよ！

This last phrase is very strong, usually only used when you really hate someone or you're about to start a fight with them!

Chikan(!)   **Chikan(!)**
ちかん（！）

Women in Japan need to watch out for **chikan**, who are strangers who enjoys doing perverse sexual acts. They like to touch any part of the woman's body, put their body against the woman's, to "flash"—and foreign women are targets as well. The **chikan** act fearlessly in public, usually riding the train during the morning and late afternoon rush hours to benefit from the closeness of the passengers. Most girls will freak out, and the few who don't might slap the offender and/or accuse him of sexual harassment. The **chikan** might counter-attack with **Dare-ga omae nanka sawaru-kayo?!** ♂ 誰がお前なんか触るかよ？！ Who would want to touch you?!

The sad part is that no one will come to the rescue—the people on the train will quietly look away as if nothing happened. If you're a guy who would like to score a few "brownie points," give your assistance in a situation like this. Everyone will be surprised—probably even more surprised than the **chikan**. But if Superman isn't around the corner, your only fallback is to use the following words/phrases and the others listed in this chapter.

Lewd! Vulgar!	Sukebe! ♀ すけべ!
Sexual perversion/ Abnormality.	Hentai. <ruby>変態<rt>へんたい</rt></ruby>。

Placing **kono** この in front of **sukebe** and **hentai** will direct the attention to one person, such as **Kono sukebe!** (You freak!) and **Kono hentai!** (You pervert!)

Take your hand(s) off!	Te dokete-yo! ♀ <ruby>手<rt>て</rt></ruby>どけてよ!
Don't touch me!	Sawan'nai-de! ♀ <ruby>触<rt>さわ</rt></ruby>んないで!
You're dirty!	Kitanai-wane! ♀ <ruby>汚<rt>きたな</rt></ruby>いわね!

Some years ago, we went to a club in Tokyo. As we were about to pay the cover charge, we were told our fee was almost twice the norm! There was no doubt in my mind as to why, but I became so irate we just left. However, the second time this happened we settled the problem right away.

If this happens to you (and it may not—some clubs see foreigners as desirable, drawing in other Japanese customers), and you are determined to patronize the place, the first thing you should do is let them know you speak and understand Japanese. That should throw them off-guard, reducing the chance of them continuing the scheme. Say anything relating to the situation, because they know what you're talking about. If they ask you questions, don't worry

about answering them. Just keep stressing what you want.
If they don't give in, do what you would do back home—
call for the manager!

But just make sure that you are actually being ripped off
before you let fly with phrases like these! Some Japanese
clubs can be very pricey, by Western and even by Japanese
standards. This is where having "local knowledge" is vital—
either gained or by having Japanese friends with you.

This can't be right!	**Kore hontō-ja nai-deshō!** ♀ これ本当じゃないでしょう！ **Kore hontō-ja nai-darō!** ♂ これ本当じゃないだろう！

This is slightly politer than the blunt phrases in *Yes and No*.
Choose your level of impact!

I think you are trying to trick me!	**Damasō-to shiteru deshō!** ♀ だまそうとしてるでしょう！ **Damasō-to shiterun-darō!** ♂ だまそうとしてるんだろう！
This can't be so expensive!	**Kon'na-ni takai-wake nai!** こんなに高い訳ない！ **Botterun-darō!** ♂ ぼってるんだろう！
This is different from what I've heard!	**Ki'ita hanashi-to chigaun dakedo!** 聞いた話と違うんだけど！

Ki'ita hanashi-to chigau-yo!
聞いた話と違うよ！

**If you think I don't
know anything,
you're wrong!**

Damasarenai-wayo! ♀
だまされないわよ！

Damasarenai-yo! ♂
だまされないよ！

Don't think I'm stupid!

Baka-ni shinai-deyo! ♀
ばかにしないでよ！

Baka-ni suruna(-yo)! ♂
ばかにするな(よ)！

Explain to me why?!

Setsumei shite?!
説明して？！

Setsumei shite-kureru?!
説明してくれる？！

Think about it!

Kangaete-mite! ♀
考えてみて！

Kangaete-mina! ♂
考えてみな！

**Don't you think
you're wrong?**

Jibun-de warui-to
omowanai-no?
自分で悪いと思わないの？

**Is this because I'm a
foreigner?**

Gaikoku-jin dakara?
外国人だから？

Is this because I'm an American?

Amerika-jin dakara?
アメリカ人だから？

I want to talk to the manager!

Manējā yon-deyo! ♀
マネージャー呼んでよ！

Manējā yonde-kure-yo! ♂
マネージャー呼んでくれよ！

I won't come here again!

Mō nido-to konai!
もう二度と来ない！

Mō nido-to konai-yo! ♂
もう二度と来ないよ！

I'll tell all my friends!

Min'na-ni iu kara!
みんなに言うから！

Min'na-ni iu zo! ♂
みんなに言うぞ！

Hey! Tell me your name!

Chotto! Namae oshiete-yo! ♀
ちょっと！名前教えてよ！

Chotto! Namae oshiero-yo! ♂
ちょっと！名前教えろよ！

**You better remember
what you tried to do!**

Oboete-nasai-yo! ♀
覚えてなさいよ！

**You won't get away
with this!**

Oboetero-yo! ♂
覚えてろよ！

13

On the Phone

Phone communication is very important to the Japanese. With transport being relatively slow in such a densely-populated country, keeping in touch electronically is the most effective way to maintain relationships. And as email has taken off a lot slower than in the West, with older generations especially, the phone is still a lifeline.

Hello(?)   **Moshi-moshi(?)**
          もしもし？

As with other often-used phrases, everyone has their own way to say **moshi-moshi**, from the musical to the interrogative. Find your style!

Is...there please? **...san-wa imaska?**
         …さんはいますか。
         ...(-wa) iru?
         …（は）いる？

Could you get...please? ...san-ni kawatte-
kuremaska?
…さんに変わってくれますか?

...ni kawatte-kureru?
…に変わってくれる?

Hold on please. Shō-shō omachi kudasai.
少々 お待ち下さい。

This is a very formal phrase, but one you might hear when a stranger answers the phone.

Chotto matte kudasai.
ちょっと待って下さい。

Chotto mattete.
ちょっと待ってて。

Calling someone's house when you don't know who might answer is one of those times you really should use the **mas** form. Calling a mobile phone of course solves this problem!

The Japanese have been the world's most enthusiastic adopters of mobile phones, with all young and more and more older people being connected. Aggressive marketing and product development mean that they have a huge choice of feature-packed **keitai denwa** 携帯電話 (usually just **keitai** 携帯), which (though of similar colors) are all light and compact with screen sizes increasing all the time. This helps with the most important feature of the phones, the text messaging, or **mēru**.

Young Japanese in particular spend hours (especially otherwise wasted time on the train) each day emailing their friends via their phones, and having one is now a necessity, not a luxury. With full and fast kanji input and low costs (usually 1 yen per message), the **mēru** culture has taken hold. And your phone is very much a form of personal expression. What trinkets you attach to it and what music plays when a call or message arrives defines who you are and what fashions you follow.

What kind of phone did you buy?	**Don'na keitai katta-no?** どんな携帯買ったの？
This (attachment) is really cute.	**Kore, sugoku kawaii.** これ、すごくかわいい。
What's your email address?	**Adoresu-wa?** アドレスは？

This is a cue for some good *katakana-ized* pronunciation practice—or frantic scribbling!

Can you do email in English/Japanese?	Eigo/Nihongo-de mēru dekiru? 英語／日本語でメールできる？
Please email me in English/Japanese?	Eigo/Nihongo-de mēru kureru? 英語／日本語でメールくれる？
It's hard to email with this phone.	Kono keitai-no mēru wakarinikui. この携帯のメール分かりにくい。
Could you teach me?	(Chotto) Oshiete-kureru? （ちょっと）教えてくれる？

But even if you **mēru** like crazy, every now and then you will still have to call someone. Here are some useful phrases.

How are you doing?	Genki? 元気？
I've been doing okay.	Genki-dayo. 元気だよ。

If you want to put these two phrases together, asking how the other person is and saying you're okay in the same breath, for clarity you should say **Genki? Atashi-wa/Boku-wa genki-dayo**, adding the subject (me) to the second phrase.

So-so/Not good, not bad.	Mā-mā. まあまあ。

What were you doing? Nani shiteta-no?
何してたの？

You're late. Osoi-ne.
遅いね。

I tried to call you. Denwa shita-noyo.
電話したのよ。

My (phone's) battery was flat. Batterī-ga kireta.
バッテリーが切れた。

The line was busy. Hanashi-chū datta.
話中だった。

Reception is bad. Denpa-ga warui.
電波が悪い。

Can you hear me? (watashi/boku-no-koe) kikoeru?
(私／僕の声)聞こえる？

I can't hear you very well.	**Yoku kikoenai** 良く聞こえない
I can't hear/ understand you at all!	**Zen-zen kikoenai!** 全然聞こえない
I'll call you back, OK?	**Kake naosu-ne?** かけ直すね？
Who was on the phone?	**Dare-ga denwa tsukatteta-no?** 誰が電話使ってたの？
I want to see you.	**Aitai.** 会いたい。
I want to see you now.	**Ima-sugu aitai.** 今すぐ会いたい。
I'll call you again.	**Mata kakeru-ne.** またかけるね。 **Mata denwa suru-ne.** また電話するね。
I'll call you after I get there (to the station).	**(Eki-ni) tsuite kara denwa suru-ne.** (駅に)着いてから電話するね。
What time can I call tomorrow?	**Ashita nanji-ni denwa shite ii?** 明日何時に電話していい？

I'll call tomorrow at 6 o'clock.

Ashita rokuji-ni denwa suru-ne.
明日6時に電話するね。

Please be home.

Ie-ni ite kudasai.
家にいて下さい。

Will you be on (Internet) chat tomorrow?

Ashita (intānetto) chatto-ni deru?
明日(インターネット)チャットに出る？

Say hello to Hisako for me.

Hisako-ni yoroshiku-ne.
ひさこによろしくね。

14

Love and Sex

I'm crazy about you.

Sugoku suki.
すごく好き。

I love you.

Aishiteru.
愛してる。

I'm yours.

Atashi-wa anata-no
mono. ♀
あたしはあなたのもの。

Boku-wa kimi-no mono. ♂
僕は君のもの。

You're mine.

Anata-wa atashi-no
mono. ♀
あなたはあたしのもの。

Kimi-wa boku-no mono ♂
君は僕のもの。

I want to know all about you.

Anata-no-koto zenbu shiritai. ♀
あなたの事全部知りたい。

Kimi-no-koto zenbu shiritai. ♂
君の事全部知りたい。

I'll tell you.

Oshiete-ageru.
教えてあげる。

You look beautiful.

Kirei-dayo.
きれいだよ。

You're attractive.

Suteki-yo.
すてきよ。

Suteki-dayo.
すてきだよ。

You're sexy!

Sekushī-dane.
セクシーだね。

Look at me.

Kotchi mite.
こっち見て。

You have beautiful eyes.

Kirei-na me-dane. ♂
きれいな目だね。

You're quiet aren't you?

Otonashii-ne?
おとなしいね?

You smell good.　　　Ii kaori.
　　　　　　　　　　　　いい香り。

May I kiss you?　　　Kisu shite-mo ii?
　　　　　　　　　　　　キスしてもいい？

Kiss me.　　　　　　Kisu shite.
　　　　　　　　　　　　キスして。

Where?　　　　　　　Doko-ni?
　　　　　　　　　　　　どこに？

May I love you?　　　Aishite-mo ii?
　　　　　　　　　　　　愛してもいい？

This has two meanings, "May I make love to you?" and
"May I give you my heart?"

Don't be shy.

Hazukashi-garanai-de.
恥ずかしがらないで。

Close your eyes.

Me-o tojite.
目を閉じて。

I'm embarrassed.

Hazukashii.
恥ずかしい。

You have a beautiful body.

Kirei-na karada-dane. ♂
きれいな体 だね。

Will you look the other way for a second?

Chotto atchi muitete?
ちょっとあっち向いてて?

Is this your first time?

Hajimete?
初めて?

Tell me the truth.

Hontō-no-koto itte.
本当の事言って。

Don't worry.

Shinpai shinai-de.
心配しないで。

It's gonna be okay.

Daijōbu(-dayo).
大丈夫(だよ)。

Treat me kindly.

Yasashiku shite-ne. ♀
優しくしてね。

Is today safe for you?

Kyō-wa daijōbu-na hi? ♂
今日は大丈夫な日?

I don't want to have a baby.	Aka-chan hoshiku-nai-no. ♀ 赤ちゃん欲しくないの。
Will you use a condom?	Gomu tsukete? ♀ ゴムつけて？
I'll use a condom.	Gomu tsukeru. ♂ ゴムつける。
Are you on the Pill?	Piru nonderu? ♂ ピル飲んでる？
I want you.	Anata-ga hoshii. ♀ あなたが欲しい。 Kimi-ga hoshii. ♂ 君が欲しい。
It's been a long time.	Hisashiburi. 久しぶり。
Love me more.	Motto aishite. もっと愛して。

More and more.	Motto motto. もっともっと。
Do the same thing again.	Mō ichido sō shite. もう一度そうして。
How do you want me to do it?	Don'na-fū-ni shite hoshii? どんなふうにして欲しい？
I feel so good.	Kimochi ii. 気持ちいい。 Sugoku ii. すごくいい。
Touch me.	Sawatte. 触って。
Bite me.	Kande. 噛んで。
Stronger/harder.	Motto tsuyoku. もっと強く。
Softer.	Motto yasashiku. もっと優しく。
Faster.	Motto hayaku. もっと速く。
Slower.	Motto yukkuri. もっとゆっくり。

Deeper.

Motto fukaku.
もっと深く。

I'm coming.

Iku iku. ♀
イク。

I'm about to come.

Iki-sō-da. ♂
イキそうだ。

Did you like (that)?

Yokatta?
よかった？

Did you come?

Itta?
イった？

That was good.

Yokatta.
よかった。
Yokatta-yo. ♂
よかったよ。

That was wonderful.

Sugoku yokatta.
すごくよかった。

One more time?

Mō ikkai?
もう一回？

I don't wanna leave you.

Hanaretaku-nai.
離れたくない。

I wanna stay with you forever.

Zutto issho-ni itai.
ずっと一緒にいたい。

Will you marry me?	Kekkon shite-kureru? 結婚してくれる?
I don't want to get married yet.	Mada kekkon shitaku-nai. まだ結婚したくない。
I don't want to get engaged yet.	Mada konyaku shitaku-nai. まだ婚約したくない。
I don't want to think about marriage yet.	Mada kekkon-nante kangaetaku-nai. まだ結婚なんて考えたくない。
I love you but I can't marry you.	Suki-dakedo kekkon-wa dekinai. 好きだけど結婚はできない。
It's not time for me to get serious.	Mada maji-ni naritaku-nai. まだマジになりたくない。
Don't get me wrong.	Gokai shinai-de. 誤解しないで。

I need time to myself.	Jibun-no jikan-ga hitsuyō-nano. ♀ 自分の時間が必要なの。 Jibun-no jikan-ga hitsuyō-nanda. ♂ 自分の時間が必要なんだ。
I'm not good for you.	Atashi-wa anata-ni fusawashiku-nai-wa. ♀ あたしはあなたにふさわしくないわ。 Boku-wa kimi-ni fusawashiku-nai-yo. ♂ 僕は君にふさわしくないよ。
Forget about me.	Atashi-no-koto wasurete. ♀ あたしの事忘れて。 Boku-no-koto wasurete. 僕の事忘れて。

Japanese terminology of intimate relations and just plain sex would take a book in itself, but here are a few common terms.

tekoki/ 手コキ hand job

anaru/ アナル anal sex

nama-de yaru/ 生でヤル to have sex without using a condom

onanī/ オナニー masturbation, (**onanī suru**: to masturbate)

dīpu kisu/ ディープキス French kiss

esu/ S sadist (both S and M are used very casually in Japan compared to in the States. Almost everyone is expected to identify either as S or M, or, **riba** reversible).

emu/ M masochist

rabuho (rabu-hoteru)/ ラブホ（ラブホテル）love hotel

yari-man/ ヤリマン slut, whore, a girl who is/perceived to be easy and/or promiscuous.

tachi/ たち a top. The person who is sexually dominant in a relationship. A term used within the gay community.

neko/ ネコ (literally "cat") a bottom. The person who is sexually submissive in a relationship. Also, うけ /**uke**. (See たち)

riba/ リバ a transliteration of "reve(rse)". Someone who can act as a top or a bottom in a sexually intimate situation, someone who is "reversible."

sōshoku-kei/ 草食系 vegetarian-type. Refers to a person who is sexually passive or indifferent.

nikushoku-kei/ 肉食系 carnivore, meat-eater-type. Refers to a person who is sexually aggressive, someone with a high sex drive.

zatshoku-kei/ 雑食系 omnivore. Refers to a person who is somewhere in the middle between a **sōshoku-kei** and **nikushoku-kei**.

uwaki/ 浮気 to cheat (**uwaki-shō**/ 浮気性 is the tendency to cheat)

furin/ 不倫 to have an affair with a married person

futamata/ 二股 to two-time

omowaseburi/ 思わせぶり suggestive, deceiving, an adjective for leading someone on/ being a tease

15

The Other Side

I'm sorry it didn't work out.	Zan'nen-dakedo atashi-tachi awanakatta-noyo. ♀ 残念だけど、あたし達合わなかったのよ。 Zan'nen-dakedo boku-tachi awanakattan-dayo. ♂ 残念だけど、僕達合わなかったんだよ。
It's over.	Mō owari-dane. もう終わりだね。 Mō owari-da. ♂ もう終わりだ。
Don't be persistent.	Shitsukoku shinai-de. ♀ しつこくしないで。 Shitsukoku suruna-yo. ♂ しつこくするなよ。

I can't see you anymore.

Mō aenai.
もう会えない。

Mō aenai-yo.
もう会えないよ。

I won't call you anymore.

Mō denwa shinai.
もう電話しない。

I don't love you anymore.

Mō suki-ja nai.
もう好きじゃない。

I have another girlfriend/boyfriend.

Hoka-ni kareshi-ga dekita-no. ♀
他に彼氏ができたの。

Hoka-ni kanojo-ga dekita. ♂
他に彼女ができた。

I'm not interested in you anymore.

Mō anata-ni kyōmi-ga nai-no. ♀
もうあなたに興味がないの。

Mō kimi-ni kyōmi-ga nain-da. ♂
もう君に興味がないんだ。

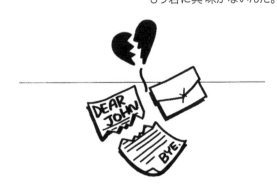

Being with you is no fun.

Issho-ni ite-mo tano-shiku-nai.
一緒にいても、楽しくない。

You're boring!

Anata tsuman'nai! ♀
あなたつまんない！

Kimi tsuman'nē! ♂
君つまんねえ！

Stop bothering me!

Jama shinai-deyo!
邪魔しないでよ！

Jama shinai-de-kure!
邪魔しないでくれ！

You don't love me anymore, do you?

Mō atashi-no-koto suki-ja nain-deshō? ♀
もうあたしの事好きじゃないんでしょう？

Mō boku-no-koto suki-ja nain-darō? ♂
もう僕の事好きじゃないんだろう？

Do you have another girlfriend/boyfriend?

Hoka-ni kanojo/kareshi-ga dekita-no?
他に彼女／彼氏ができたの？

Please tell me. I want to know.

Oshiete. Shiritai-no. ♀
教えて。知りたいの。

Oshiete. Shiritain-da. ♂
教えて。知りたいんだ。

I'm sorry I haven't been a good girlfriend/boyfriend.

Ii kanojo-janakute gomen-ne. ♀
いい彼女じゃなくてごめんね。

Ii kareshi-janakute gomen. ♂
いい彼氏じゃなくてごめん。

It's my fault.

Atashi-ga warui-no. ♀
あたしが悪いの。

Boku-no sei. ♂
僕のせい。

Can't we start again?

Mō ichido yarinaose-nai?
もう一度やり直せない？

I'm serious about you.

Anata-no-koto honki-nano. ♀
あなたの事本気なの。

Kimi-no-koto maji/honki-nanda. ♂
君の事マジ／本気なんだ。

I can't live without you.

Anata nashi-ja ikiteke-nai. ♀
あなたなしじゃ生きてけない。

Kimi nashi-ja ikiteke-nai. ♂
君なしじゃ生きてけない。

Please understand my feelings.	Atashi-no kimochi wakatte. ♀ あたしの気持ち分かって。 Boku-no kimochi wakatte. ♂ 僕の気持ち分かって。
I will never forget you.	Anata-no-koto wasure-nai. ♀ あなたの事忘れない。 Kimi-no-koto wasure-nai. ♂ 君の事忘れない。
Thanks for the beautiful memories.	Ii omoide-o arigatō. いい思い出をありがとう。
I'm so happy to have known you.	Shiriaete/Deaete yokatta. 知り合えて／出合えてよかった。
Remember me sometimes.	Tokidoki atashi-no-koto omoidashite. ♀ 時々あたしの事思い出して。 Tokidoki boku-no-koto omoidashite. ♂ 時々僕の事思い出して。
Can we still be friends?	Mada tomodachi-de irareru? まだ友達でいられる？
Be happy with her/him.	Kanojo/kare-to shiawase-nine. 彼女／彼と幸せにね。

I loved you.

Aishiteta. ♀
愛してた。

Aishiteta-yo. ♂
愛してたよ。

I will always love you.

Zutto anata-o omotteru. ♀
ずっとあなたを思ってる。

Zutto kimi-o omotteru. ♂
ずっと君を思ってる。

I really don't love you anymore, so I'm going to change my phone number.

Mō suki-ja nai-kara, denwa bangō kaeru.
もう好きじゃないから電話番号変える。

It's not you, it's me.

Kimi-no sei-ja nai, boku-no sei-dayo. ♀
君のせいじゃない、僕のせいだよ。

Anata-no sei-ja nai, watashi-no sei-yo. ♂
あなたのせいじゃない、私のせいよ。

I can't believe you're doing this to me.

Kon'na-koto suru-nante, shinji-rarenai.
こんな事するなんて、信じられない。

Forget it!

Yameta!
止めた！

I'll miss you.

Sabishiku-naru-yo.
寂しくなるよ。

I'll always think of you.

Itsumo anata-o omotteru-wa. ♀
いつもあなたを思ってるわ。

Itsumo kimi-o omotteru-yo. ♂
いつも君を思ってるよ。

I'll always love you.

Itsumo suki. ♀
いつも好き。

Itsumo suki-dayo. ♂
いつも好きだよ。

I'll write letters.

Tegami kaku-yo.
手紙書くよ。

Will you write me a letter?

Tegami kureru?
手紙くれる？

I'll call you from Thailand.

Tai-kara denwa suru.
タイから電話する。

I'll call you when I return.

Kaette-kitara denwa suru.
帰って来たら電話する。

I'll be back soon.	Sugu kaette-kuru. すぐ帰って来る。 Sugu kaette-kuru-yo. すぐ帰って来るよ。
Please understand.	(Dōka) wakatte. (どうか)分かって。
I have to go because it's my job.	Shigoto dakara ikanakucha. 仕事だから行かなくちゃ。
Take care of yourself.	Genki-dene. 元気でね。
Please wait for my return.	Mattete-ne. 待っててね。

You can use this anytime—when leaving your house, going to the restroom, getting a drink at the bar…

Don't cry.	Nakanai-de. 泣かないで。
Wipe your tears.	Namida fuite. 涙ふいて。
I can't stand it!	Gaman dekinai! 我慢できない! Gaman dekinai-yo! 我慢できないよ!

Taerarenai!
耐えられない！

Taerarenai-yo!
耐えられないよ！

All of these phrases can be used for both sad and mad feelings.

It's difficult for me too. **Atashi-mo tsurai-wa.** ♀
あたしも辛いわ。

Boku-mo tsurain-da. ♂
僕も辛いんだ。